India - A World Leader In Cow Killing And Beef Export

An Italian Did It In 10 Years

What The British Could Not Do in 200 Years And The Muslims In 800 Years

By
Dr. Sahadeva dasa

B.com., FCA., AICWA., PhD
Chartered Accountant

Soul Science University Press

Abridged Version of The Book - Cow Killing And Beef Export - The Master Plan To Turn India Into A Desert (Section1)

www.cowism.com

Readers interested in the subject matter of this
book are invited to correspond with the publisher at:
SoulScienceUniversity@gmail.com   +91 98490 95990
or visit DrDasa.com

First Edition: July 2013

Soul Science University Press expresses its gratitude to the
Bhaktivedanta Book Trust International (BBT), for the use of quotes by
His Divine Grace A.C.Bhaktivedanta Swami Prabhupada.

ISBN 97893-82947-17-2

Published by:
Dr. Sahadeva dasa for Soul Science University Press

Printed by:
Rainbow Print Pack, Hyderabad

To order a copy write to purnabramhadasa@gmail.com
or buy online: Amazon.com, rlbdeshop.com

Contents

Preface
1. Beef Exports Up 44% In 4 Years 9
2. Transforming A Nation With The Lowest Meat
   Consumption In The World 12
3. Massive Nationwide Drive - To Establish New
   Slaughterhouses And Modernize Existing Ones 18
4. Pink Revolution - A Historic Policy Shift,
   Unprecedented In India's History 42
5. Subsidies And Tax Rebates - On Meat Processing
   And Export 62
6. Rail Minister Signs Order To Resume Cow
   Carriage Trains 67
7. White Lies And Blatant Cover-ups 73
8. Factory Farms Coming To India In A Big Way 77
9. Government's Push For Livestock Business -
   Killing The Soul Of The Nation 86
10. Promoting Export Of Meat Will Kill
    Livestock-Driven Farming 93
11. Rant To Legalize Cattle Smuggling On
    Bangladesh Border 97
12. India-Pak Livestock Export Deal 100
13. Recognition And Awards To Meat Exporters 103
14. Locking Horns Over Culture And Business 106
15. The New Livestock Policy - A Policy Of
    Ecocide Of Indigenous Cattle Breeds And
    A Policy Of Genocide For India's Small Farms 111
16. Cow Raids - The Most Lucrative Profession In India . . 124
The Author

Preface

May 2004 marked a significant moment in Indian history when a newly elected government decided to accord highest priority to beef consumption and export, making it 'truly a national initiative'.

India is known all over the world as a peace loving country. It is a historical fact that India has never attacked any other nation and has always believed in the philosophy of peaceful coexistence.

It is also probably the only country that provides for animal care in its constitution. Animals are mentioned as something more than just food. Each citizen is enjoined to care for and preserve nature and its creatures.

Article 48, The Directive Principles of State Policy states, "The state shall, in particular, take steps for … prohibiting the slaughter of cows and calves and other milch and draught cattle."

India has been a country of farmers and shepherds, lovingly looking after their animals. India was never a country of butchers and murderers. Bloodbath is foreign to Indian culture.

Compassion and non-violence formed the core belief of all the religions that originated from this great land.

Traditional Indian or Vedic way of life teaches respect for all life forms. In their view, all living beings are born of mother nature and have an equal right to life. Indeed, in Vedic conception, animals are treated like innocent children and are meant to be given all protection.

Srimad Bhagavatam, the foremost of all Vedic texts states, "One should treat animals such as deer, camels, asses, monkeys, mice, snakes, birds and flies exactly like one's own son. How little difference there actually is between children and these innocent animals." (SB 7.14.9)

But suddenly India's national policy took a U-turn when a particular political party came to power. It was a significant moment in the history of this great nation.

Website of the Ministry of Food Processing Industries stated:

"There is an urgent need to frame a right strategy for the development of meat and poultry production in the country. This will certainly bring prosperity to millions of our rural citizens and create employment in rural India. Having achieved the Green Revolution, the White Revolution and the Blue Revolution, it is time to ask the question "can the Pink Revolution be far behind?" Certainly this will require large investment in infrastructure, mainly in cold storages, and modern meat processing plants. Without a strong and dependable cold chain, a vital sector like meat industry, which is based mostly on perishable products, cannot survive and grow."

They relentlessly pursued their agenda for a decade and the crowning success came when India became the top seller of beef in 2013.

But this nation will pay a great price for this great mischief by its leaders. This heinous crime against creation will never go unpunished by the stringent laws of nature.

Sahadeva dasa

Dr. Sahadeva dasa
1st June 2013
Secunderabad, India

Beef Exports Up 44% In 4 Years

India Is Top Seller In The World

According to a Times of India report dated April 1, 2013, India, homeland of the sacred cow has become the world's leading beef exporter in 2013. Last year itself, USDA's Foreign Agricultural Service forecasts showed that India would ship roughly 1.5 million metric tons of beef, passing reigning export champion Australia. It's a remarkable rise from just three years ago, when this famously bovine-friendly country exported less than half that amount.

The Central government's Pink Revolution to promote meat production and export has led to a 44% increase in meat consumption and export in four years, but it has failed to regulate the industry.

It certainly seems surprising at first, that a nation widely known for revering the cow would be a beef exporter at all.

According to data compiled by the animal husbandry departments of all states, meat from registered slaughterhouses increased from 5.57 lakh tonnes in 2008 to 8.05 lakh tonnes in 2011. Export earnings from bovine (beef and cattle) meat touched Rs 18,000 crore in 2012-2013.

Indian beef exports for 2012 were forecast at 1.525 million MT, 25% higher than the previous year and an almost three fold increase in the past 10 years.

Though beef meeting international standards reaches markets in the Europe, the Gulf and South-East Asia, the way animals are transported and slaughtered is extremely cruel and far from international standards. "There is rampant abuse of animals in transport and slaughter of meat whether for domestic consumption or export," says Arpan Sharma, CEO of Federation of Indian Animal Protection Organisations.

India's Central government has taken up modernization of abattoirs and storage facilities on a war footing. The food processing ministry announced subsidies of over 4000 crores to modernize abattoirs.

There are 38 integrated abattoirs in the country which slaughter for export. This is apart from thousands of other abattoirs which are operating unofficially. Agricultural and Processed Food Exports Development Authority (APEDA) is responsible for overseeing their operations.

None of the meat exporters pay attention to the condition of animals. Crammed in lorries, the animals are transported without

Himalayan Academy explains it:

The cow represents the giving nature of life to every Hindu. Honoring this gentle animal, who gives more than she takes, we honor all creatures. Hindus regard all living creatures as sacred—mammals, fishes, birds and more. We acknowledge this reverence for life in our special affection for the cow. At festivals we decorate and honor her. To the Hindu, the cow symbolizes all other creatures. The cow is a symbol of the Earth, the nourisher, the ever-giving, undemanding provider. The cow represents life and the sustenance of life. The cow is so generous, taking nothing but water, grass and grain. She gives and gives and gives of her milk, as does the liberated soul gives of his spiritual knowledge. The cow is so vital to life, the virtual sustainer of life, for many humans. The cow is a symbol of grace and abundance. Veneration of the cow instills in Hindus the virtues of gentleness, receptivity and connectedness with nature.

food and water. Police officers let vehicles through without fining them for overloading as per the Prevention of Cruelty to Animals Act.

The international practice of stunning an animal before slaughter is not followed in India. In Kerala, cows are killed by hammer blows.

India overtakes Australia, Brazil, and the United States in beef export, in that order. Each of those nations will export around 1.2-1.4m metric tons of beef this year. India's beef is mostly sold in the Middle East, North Africa, and Southeast Asia with some portion going to European nations.

International community is shocked that a nation in which cow slaughter is officially prohibited and is an utter anathema to the majority of the population, will overtake these three icons (Australia, Brazil and US) of cattle ranching and beef eating.

This is just an indication of the efforts and planning the central government is putting in to accomplish this 'feat'.

> *yas tvam krsne gate duram saha-gandiva-dhanvana*
> *socyo'sy asocyan rahasi praharan vadham arhasi*
>
> *You rogue, do you dare beat an innocent cow because Lord Krsna and Arjuna, the carrier of the Gandiva bow, are out of sight? Since you are beating the innocent in a secluded place, you are considered a culprit and therefore deserve to be killed.*
>
> *In a civilization where God is conspicuously banished, and there is no devotee warrior like Arjuna, the associates of the age of Kali take advantage of this lawless kingdom and arrange to kill innocent animals like the cow in secluded slaughterhouses. Such murderers of animals stand to be condemned to death by the order of a pious king like Maharaja Pariksit. For a pious king, the culprit who kills an animal in a secluded place is punishable by the death penalty, exactly like a murderer who kills an innocent child in a secluded place.*
>
> *~ Srimad Bhagavatam 9.2.3*

2.

Transforming A Nation

With The Lowest Meat Consumption In The World

According to a report by Rachel Tepper in Huffington Post, Indian meat consumption is lowest in the world, at only seven pounds per person a year.

Tiny European nation Luxembourg tips the scales at 136.5 kg of meat per person a year, or roughly 300 pounds, and occupies the first place in meat consumption. Burger-loving U.S. comes second.

The information, gathered by the U.N. Food And Agriculture Organization (FAO) and analyzed by The Economist, indicates that consumption of meat has been on the rise worldwide over the last 50 years. 177 countries were included in the study.

Tastes have changed, too:

Cow (beef and veal) was top of the menu in the early 1960s, accounting for 40% of meat consumption, but by 2007 its share had fallen to 23%. Pig is now the animal of choice, with around 99m tonnes consumed.

Although Western countries still eat the most meat per person, The Economist notes that it's middle-income countries like China that drive worldwide demand for it.

In addition to being linked to health problems, meat consumption has environmental experts crying foul. In 2008, Time reported that FAO data indicates that 18 percent of the Earth's greenhouse gas emissions were linked to worldwide livestock farming. In contrast, emissions from cars, trains, planes and boats worldwide combined accounted for only 13 percent.

As the world wakes up to the dangers of meat eating and a wave of vegetarianism sweeps through the world, Indian government realizes it's time to promote meat consumption and export. They are going out of their way to get the vegetarian population hooked on to taste of meat.

Policy makers have no regard for India's native food culture, which is one of the richest in the world. They are rolling-out red carpet welcome to western fast food chains.

Of the 7 billion people on the planet, nearly 1.2 billion of them are Indians and if this segment of humanity starts eating meat on American scale, its environmental, economic and moral implications will be catastrophic.

The Race To Make A Meal Of India's Fast-Food Market

When Domino's Pizza Inc. came to India in 1996 – in the first wave of international fast-food brands to enter the country – the company had to start with some basic education of its market.

They had to teach, 'This is a pizza and it's made from ingredients you are familiar with, but the shape is different.' Indians embraced it, enthusiastically enough that Domino's now has 513 outlets across 112 cities in India, with a restaurant and delivery business. But a couple of years ago, Domino's concluded it needed to start a second round of vigorous education: Convincing a new group of Indians that they belong in restaurants.

Domino's, working through its master franchisee Jubilant FoodWorks Ltd., put its product developers to work designing a

> *The whole process of westernizing, India or materializing India began about two hundred years ago. The Westerners introduced their so-called civilization, with its coffee, tea and meat eating. They built factories and developed large cities that had never been developed before. The entire Indian economy had been based on the villages, but under British rule and then recently more and more, everything moved towards the city. What happened is that the Vedic culture broke down. When it was present, the necessities of life were plentiful; there was no difficulty. But by and by it broke down.*
> *~ Srila Prabhupada (A Cheating Civilization)*

pizza they could sell for under a dollar. The big savings came in cheese, when the company replaced mozzarella with what it calls "liquid cheese sauce." In 2008, Domino's India launched its first Pizzamania, priced at 35 rupees (about 65 cents).

It opened doors for a lot of Indians who had never tried Domino's or ordered us at home," Mr. Rajpal, CEO says. "We see a lot of new people who had never tried pizza coming to us – and over time graduating to other products. … It's democratic consumption now."

This strategy is also being aggressively pursued by the other big players in the $12.5-billion Indian fast-food industry. While organized retail has only 5 per cent of the fast-food market, it is growing with explosive speed, about 36 per cent last year, dominated by a handful of international brands.

McDonald's Corp. is the clear leader, according to a market analysis by Euromonitor released in October, with 2 per cent of the quick-service market. Pizza Hut Inc. and KFC Corp. – which, like McDonald's and Domino's, entered India in 1996 – each have close to 250 outlets. Subway, which arrived in 2002, is playing a fast game of catch-up with 320 stores in 60 cities and plans to top 400 sites next year; Baskin-Robbins has locked up the dessert market, with 425 stores in 95 cities, including many far from the country's major urban hubs.

All of these firms have relied on the international cachet of their brands to get people in the store.

And all are now using a "sub-dollar pricing" strategy to try to convince a new segment of consumers that regular visits to a fast-food outlet are feasible for them.

KFC has been the market leader here, with a "Streetwise" range offering a hot chicken meal starting from 25 rupees. Domino's Pizzamania is now priced at 44 rupees. McDonald's offers a full hot lunch for under a dollar. Pizza Hut has 60-cent "iPan" pizzas for delivery.

Subway, which struggled initially because of the higher cost of its ingredients, this year experimented with a "toastie," a 60-cent open-face sandwich, that marketing manager Sanjiv Pandey says appeals both to Indians' love of hot food and the low-budget market. "It is a phenomenal entry level price point and it's worked fantastically well for us."

All of this ultralow pricing is paired with aggressive print and television marketing, showing people who clearly cover a wide socioeconomic range eating in the outlets.

Domino's pioneered delivery, startling customers with its "30 minutes or it's free" promise (a massive logistics achievement in cities such as New Delhi and Mumbai that regularly experience total traffic gridlock). McDonald's has since taken the lead in delivery, with a 24-hour call centre and online ordering. It has also been the first to experiment with drive-throughs and gas-station outlets.

So people are becoming meat-eaters nowadays. There is no secrecy. Formerly, at least in India, the meat-eaters used to eat meat very secretly. We had seen in our childhood. If somebody will meat-eat, it was not allowed within the house. They, formerly, rich men, they used to keep Muslim servants as the caretaker of the horse or the carriage driver. So in the horse stable they would secretly cook some meat, and the so-called Babu, Zamindar, will eat. It was not allowed. And those who are not rich men -- poor men, sudra class -- they would go to Kali-ghata, and get one goat, sacrifice there, and cook there and eat, then come back. Meat-eating was not at all allowed. The higher caste, especially the brahmanas, they would never touch. Still in some provinces, in Maharastra provinces, in Madras... Of course, they are now taking.

So meat-eaters means mleccha. So now that is increasing, meat-eaters. So when wholesale population will be meat-eaters, mleccha, they'll not understand anything about spiritual matter -- "Why it is forbidden?" Because the meat-eaters, they cannot understand anything about spiritual matter. It is very difficult for them. ~Srila Prabhupada (Lecture, Srimad-Bhagavatam 1.8.34 -- Mayapur, October 14, 1974)

The Scramble To Enter India Intensifies

Several U.S. chains have announced plans to enter the country, hoping to tap the growing fast-food market.

Restaurants like Denny's Corp , known for serving pancakes and sausages all day and Pollo Tropical of Carrols Restaurant , known for Caribbean-flavored chicken, Applebee's and Johnny Rockets, known for its hamburgers, are also looking to cash into the Indian quick-service restaurant market.

All brands will face challenges as they compete with incumbent McDonald's and Yum Brands, not the least of which would be adapting a meat-centric menu to a largely vegetarian palate.

Others wanting a foothold include Wendy's, Arby's International, CKE Restaurants with Carl's Jr and Focus Brands with Schlotzsky's Deli, all known for sandwiches and burgers.

Also India may finally get to savour Ikea meat balls. The Swedish giant has all the necessary permissions to set up their furniture showroom and restaurants in India.

BannaStrow's Crepes and Coffee, Moe's Southwest Grill, Starbucks Corp, Dunkin Donuts and Carvel Ice Cream are also in line.

These franchise owners are queuing up at the Ministry of Commerce and Industry and the Ministry of Corporate Affairs. It is not difficult to get a license issued, as long as you are willing to grease a few palms.

When I think about how "fast food" came to be, I think it definitely destroys the art of traditional cooking. Fast food changes the nutritional value and flavor of food. It has to be mass produced to feed so many people (although a lot of food gets thrown away by restaurants). It has to be made in a way so it can be shipped all over the country and then prepared in 5 minutes to eat. A lot of McDonald's food products aren't even real food. They put fillers in the meats with flavor enhancers. Subway has fake chicken and their bread is so cheap it goes bad within hours after being made (it becomes hard as a rock by the end of the day, I use to work at a few subways).

The basic food culture in many countries is actually healthy. The fast food chains sell all but healthy food. Also they puts family owned eateries out of business. ~ Amber Toebosis

Waistlines Surge With A Surging Market

But the increasing consumption of processed food that is high in fat and sugar is causing worries that India is importing the Western disease of obesity, creating a ticking public health bomb that the country can ill-afford.

While undernutrition is rampant – more than 50 percent of children are stunted due to malnutrition, according to a 2008 study in The Lancet medical journal – the over-fed middle class is growing in numbers and in trouser sizes.

A November 2010 study by the National Diabetes, Obesity and Cholesterol Foundation of India found that one in three children in private schools in New Delhi were obese, compared with one in 10 in government schools. Schoolchildren are attracted to the way junk food is advertised. Fast food giants are specifically targeting them.

3.

Massive Nationwide Drive

To Establish New Slaughterhouses And Modernize/Expand Existing Slaughterhouses

Present Indian government came to power 10 years ago. After assuming office, their first move was to modernize existing slaughterhouses and grant licenses for establishing new slaughterhouses. A lucrative subsidy ranging from 50-90% was offered to lure entrepreneurs in this area. Contacts were established with slaughterhouse machinery suppliers in Europe and China. The whole government machinery was mobilized to usher in a new era of increased meat consumption and export. It was a significant policy shift in last several centuries. Even the British in their 200 years of rule could not accomplish what the present government has accomplished in just 10 years. It helps to have an Italian brain at the top and an agriculture minister who is practically a butcher himself, owning several piggeries and poultries.

This team was able to fulfill the dream of India's founders like Pandit Nehru who can finally rest in peace now. It was their cherished desire to see Indians eat, drink and have sex like Westerners. These founders must be reveling in their graves, having fulfilled their long pending dreams. After independence, it took Indian leaders 65 long years to accomplish this feat.

There's Method In Madness - Targeting The Rural Population

As we saw in the previous chapter, urban population is being 'taken care of' by multinational fast food chains but transforming rural population has presented a considerable challenge.

In India, rural diet mostly consists of locally grown farm products and meat consumption, when compared to cities, is very low. But this is all set to change. Majority of Indian population still lives in villages and smaller towns and the government has decided to target them as potential consumers. And this is no small number - we are talking of 700 million people here, that is 10% of humanity. It's hard to calculate the environmental, health and economic cost of a move of this sort.

A Central Government circular is produced below to give the readers an idea of their modus operandi.

Circular No. 217 /ICD - 44/2009
24 December 2009
The Chairman / Managing Director
All Scheduled Commercial Banks /
All Scheduled (Primary) Urban Cooperative Banks
All RRBs/ADFCs/SCBs/SCARDBs
All other institutions eligible for NABARD refinance

Dear Sir
Centrally Sponsored Scheme - Establishment/Modernisation of Rural Slaughter Houses

As you are aware, meat industry in India has great potential but received very limited attention for its growth and development due to socio-religious factors. Slaughter houses have been under the control of municipal authorities/local bodies but no systematic efforts have been made so far to make meat production a commercial activity. Barring a few export-oriented abattoirs, it has been in the hands of those who have no knowledge of slaughter house hygiene, sanitation and meat quality.

> *Thus when there is a demoniac rule, everything concerning the Vedic principles is turned upside down, all the religious ceremonies of yajna are stopped, the resources meant to be spent for yajna are taken away by the demoniac government, everything becomes chaotic, and consequently the entire world becomes hell itself.*
> ~ Srila Prabhupada (Srimad Bhagavatam 7.8.44)

2. In this background, it has been decided by Government of India to launch a subsidy based credit linked scheme for establishment/ modernisation of Rural Slaughter Houses on pilot basis during the remaining period of XI Five Year Plan with effect from 2009-10 in three States, viz., Andhra Pradesh, Meghalaya and Uttar Pradesh. The credit linked back-ended subsidy shall be provided on the total financial outlay for the sub-sectors as indicated at para 6.1 of the guidelines.

3. The assistance under the scheme shall be available to any company, partnership firm, NGO and individual entrepreneurs. Capital subsidy @ 50% of the total financial outaly of the project with the upper ceiling as indicated in para 6.1 and 6.2 of the guidelines shall be available for all categories of the promoters.

4. The Department of Animal Husbandry, Dairying and Fisheries, Ministry of Agriculture, Government of India, is the focal department for the scheme. NABARD will be administering the subsidy and monitoring the progress of the scheme besides providing refinance support to the eligible financing banks for the term loan extended under the scheme. Extent and interest rate of refinance will be as per instructions issued by NABARD from time to time.

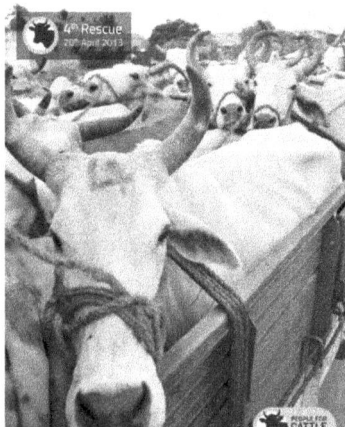

5. The implementation of the scheme shall be monitored by the Central Monitoring Committee (CMC) on a half yearly basis and the State Level Sanctioning and Monitoring Committee (SLSMC) will review the progress on quarterly basis. The participating banks will conduct periodic inspections of the units and give a feedback to the SLSMC on a consolidated basis.

6. The SLSMCs in each State are expected to meet quickly after their constitution and decide whether proposal concerning each beneficiary is to be placed before the Committee for approval or proposals of a district/cluster are to be firmed up and bunched together for consideration of the Committee or the Committee would ratify the action taken by the financial institution on individual projects.

7. We request you to circulate the operational guidelines among your controlling offices and branches in the concerned states with instructions to implement the scheme expeditiously and advise your Controlling offices to submit the proposals to the Regional Offices of NABARD in the respective states. NABARD will release subsidy subject to availability of funds from GoI. You may also take steps for giving wide publicity to the scheme. The State Animal Husbandry Department may also be approached for popularising the scheme and mobilising applications from prospective promoters. A copy of the operational guidelines of the scheme is enclosed. English and Hindi versions of the operational guidelines would be placed in the website of NABARD

Please acknowledge receipt.

Yours faithfully

(S C Kaushik)

Chief General Manager

Guidelines For Establishment /Modernisation Of
Rural Slaughter Houses

1. Background

Meat sector is one of the poorly organised sectors in our country. Though the consumption of meat is on the increase, the quality aspects have remained unchanged. Slaughterhouses have been under the control of municipal authorities and no effort had been made to make meat production an economic activity. Lack of finance, poor private participation, and environmental problems are some of the other constraints felt.

It is not just the cow slaughter business that is disturbing. The cruelty of animal transport in India is mind boggling. It would never be permitted by the beef-eaters in the US or EU where strict laws regarding movement of animals by road or train are enforced. I have seen French police stop trucks going into Spain and make the attendants feed and water the cattle before proceeding (that was in the 1960s; the rules are much stricter today). Today I see trucks sneak through the back roads of my town with cows with broken legs dangling off the back of the vehicle as they head for Pondicherry and Chennai.

~ Dinesh Wadhwa, Goa

1.2 With enactment of Food Safety and Standards Act 2006, all the food items produced in the country will have to meet a certain level of quality standards in terms of hygiene prescribed. Meat is probably one item, which has not been paid adequate attention in this regard. At present slaughter houses in rural areas are under the control of local bodies like Panchayats and Municipalities. The slaughterhouses maintained by them get least priority and no standards are being

> *ma saurabheyatra suco*
> *vyetu te vrsalad bhayam*
> *ma rodir amba bhadram te*
> *khalanam mayi sastari*
>
> *O son of Surabhi, you need lament no longer now. There is no need to fear this low-class sudra. And, O mother cow, as long as I am living as the ruler and subduer of all envious men, there is no cause for you to cry. Everything will be good for you.*
>
> *Protection of bulls and cows and all other animals can be possible only when there is a state ruled by an executive head like Maharaja Pariksit. Maharaja Pariksit addresses the cow as mother, for he is a cultured, twice-born, ksatriya king. Surabhi is the name of the cows which exist in the spiritual planets and are especially reared by Lord Sri Krsna Himself. As men are made after the form and features of the Supreme Lord, so also the cows are made after the form and features of the surabhi cows in the spiritual kingdom. In the material world the human society gives all protection to the human being, but there is no law to protect the descendants of Surabhi, who can give all protection to men by supplying the miracle food, milk. But Maharaja Pariksit and the Pandavas were fully conscious of the importance of the cow and bull, and they were prepared to punish the cow-killer with all chastisement, including death. There has sometimes been agitation for the protection of the cow, but for want of pious executive heads and suitable laws, the cow and the bull are not given protection. The human society should recognize the importance of the cow and the bull and thus give all protection to these important animals, following in the footsteps of Maharaja Pariksit. For protecting the cows and brahminical culture, the Lord, who is very kind to the cow and the saintly persons, will be pleased with us and will bestow upon us real peace.*
>
> *~ Srimad Bhagavatam 1.17.9*

insisted on. Production of meat in them cannot be recognized as meat from organized sector.

Schemes to improve slaughterhouses formulated in the past have not been very effective, since most of them concentrated on large urban-based slaughterhouses. Even at present, Ministry of Food Processing has prepared a scheme to support large modern slaughterhouses for supply of meat to cities. These will be units of large outlay and help produce wholesome meat for the consumers in these cities.

1.3 To make this sector dynamic, targeting large slaughterhouses will not suffice. Addition of value at the local level will be more ideal, as it will limit transport of animals, contain environmental pollution to local levels, and help animal owners to earn better income by providing them direct access to market. It is important to introduce private participation and make the activity a business. The past shows that slaughterhouses at industrial scale have been successful only in the private sector where they are run as meat producing centres.

1.4 Service slaughterhouses have not been self-sustaining, as the service charges collected do not meet even the running expenses leading to maintenance of units. Small slaughterhouses have not been tried on commercial lines, except in few cases and even in them no systemic investments have been made. A pilot scheme to encourage establishment of rural slaughterhouses and help entrepreneurs to undertake the activity as a bankable venture is envisaged.

2. Objectives of the Scheme

i.   To establish a new system of slaughter of livestock along with network of cold chain and distribution on commercial basis.

ii. To develop models of slaughterhouses which can be run by private entrepreneurs in rural and semi urban areas with population of less than 50,000.

iii. To encourage value addition to the products in rural areas so that livestock owners get better income and wastage of byproducts of slaughterhouses is avoided.

iv. To ensure hygiene in meat production from the slaughterhouse to consumer table by establishing cold chain and distribution system.

v.   Minimize clandestine slaughter and provide pollution free environment.

3. Definition

For the purpose of the scheme, rural slaughter houses are those which are located in places with a population of less than 50,000.

4. Implementing period and Area of Operation

The pilot phase will be implemented during the remaining XI plan period in three states viz. Andhra Pradesh, Meghalaya and Uttar Pradesh on a first come first serve basis.

5. Eligibility

5.1. Any company, partnership firm, NGO and individual entrepreneur would be eligible for the assistance if they set up/ modernize the slaughter houses / poultry dressing units as per guidelines laid down. They should have the necessary approval of the local body to take up the work.

5.2. Each entrepreneur would be eligible to avail benefit under the scheme for two units per State with a ceiling of four units under the scheme.

All possible care will be taken to avoid duplication of projects under the scheme with similar projects implemented by Ministry of Food Processing Industries in the same areas.

A signboard displaying "Assisted by Department of Animal Husbandry Dairying and Fisheries, Ministry of Agriculture, Government of India" will be exhibited at the unit.

After reproducing this government circular, now we present several media reports on modernization and expansion of slaughterhouse activities in India.

Hi-Tech Killing In The Ancient City Of Patna

Times News Network | Dec 11, 2012,

If things go according to plans, Patna may soon have a hi-tech slaughter house. An expression of interest on the website of Bihar Urban Infrastructure Development Corporation Limited (BUIDCO) has been posted about setting up a modern slaughter house on a five-acre plot at Rama Chakberia on Patna-Gaya Road. The estimated cost of the slaughter house would be Rs 26.34 crore.

The proposed structure would have the capacity of slaughtering 200 cattle besides 350 sheep and goat on eight-hour shift basis. Ministry of Food Processing Industry, Government of India (MoFPI), has approved Rs 11 crore grant for the project. The bidders can avail the grant subject to the condition that it meets the MoFPI guidelines.

According to the proposal, the selected agency would have to set up backward linkage and livestock reception yard, a lairage, slaughter lines for sheep, goat and cows, effluent treatment plant (ETP), dry rendering plant, forward linkage with meat, transport facility under cold chain system and meat packaging plant. To keep the plant and adjoining areas healthy, the agency would have to install a rendering-cum-carcass utilization plant for disposal of cadavers and meat waste.

However, BUIDCO managing director Anupam Kumar Suman says, "The project has to be implemented in 24 months. It is a semi-mechanized project but the agency would be free to install a fully mechanized plant."

Earlier, Patna Municipal Corporation (PMC) had constructed a boundary wall around the allotted land but due to the local residents' protest they had failed to proceed with the project. The slaughter house will be made under public private partnership (PPP) mode.

PMC maintains one goat abattoir near Ashok Cinema. "Maintaining a goat abattoir is far easier than providing hygiene to the cow abattoir. The existing cow abattoir runs in an unhealthy and unhygienic condition and there is no option than to shift it," says PMC commissioner Pankaj Kumar Pal.

---

pravrttim ca nivrttim ca
jana na vidur asurah
na saucam napi cacaro
na satyam tesu vidyate

"Those who are demonic do not know what is to be done and what is not to be done. Neither cleanliness nor proper behavior nor truth is found in them" (Bhagavad-gita 16.7).

Because demons do not know what to do and what not to do, they become involved in unclean dealings. As clearly indicated in the Bhagavad-gita, these are classic symptoms of a demonic personality. As long as such demons falsely occupy responsible government posts, the people in general will not be peaceful, prosperous, or happy.
~ Srila Prabhupada (Back To Godhead, 12-7, 1977)

Proposed Ultra Modern Slaughter House For Shimla, The Queen Of Hills

http://www.shimlamc.gov.in/page/Slaughter-House.aspx

The present slaughterhouse is existing since British days and happens to be one of the oldest slaughterhouse in the country. It is in a dilapidated condition. The existing site is not connected to a proper road where trucks/ load wagons can ply. Moreover this site is thickly inhabited and when the meat is transported on head load by coolies, there is resentment amongst the locals.

It is difficult to clean blood and excreta from old floors and walls. Moreover hides are removed manually. Effluent from the existing slaughterhouse is going untreated into the sewerage system and the adjoining nalah.

Considering these demerits, Ministry of Agriculture approved modernization of this slaughterhouse on 50:50 basis.

Project submitted amounted to Rs.19.43 crores. Later the Ministry of Food Processing Industries consented to provide 33% of the project cost or 4.00 Crores whichever was less. Since the tenders amounting to Rs. 13.65 Crores had been finalized hence the balance amount was to be provided by the H.P. Govt. or from any other sources.

Long, Cruel Road To The Slaughterhouse
Bindiya Chari, Times News Network, May 2, 2013,
A committee constituted by the high court of Bombay at Goa has discovered that animals brought to Goa from neighbouring states for slaughtering, often face cruelty during transportation. Animals get injured as vehicles carrying them from Karnataka and Maharashtra are packed beyond their intended capacity.

And if animals are unable stand due to injuries before the slaughter, meat traders put chilli powder in their eyes, says the report.

Meat traders brought animals to Goa without transportation certificate though it is mandatory under the Animal transportation Rules 1978. Animals are slaughtered at the state-run slaughter house, Goa meat complex (GMC) at Usgao in Ponda.

In The Holy City Of Varanasi, Slaughter Houses Get Funds For Modernisation

Rajeev Dikshit, Times News Network, Mar 22, 2013,

Opening of a modern slaughter house to replace old and now closed Kamalgadaha slaughter house will not be done before the end of the current financial year. But the funds to modernize the existing low capacity slaughter houses at Orderly Bazaar and Beniabag have been released.

Municipal commissioner RP Singh said that due to directives of the ministry of environment, Varanasi Municipal Corporation (VMC) has allowed low capacity slaughter houses at Orderly Bazaar and Beniabag to operate till a modern slaughterhouse opens.

Municipal veterinary officer Mohammad Aslam Ansari said that only small animals are butchered at Beniabag while Orderly Bazaar also slaughters big animals. He said that the divisional commissioner had recently sanctioned a budget of Rs 91 lakh to establish bio-digesters at both these slaughter houses. A fund of Rs 5 lakh had also been released for the renovation of Beniabag slaughter house. A proposal of Rs 1.5 crore had been submitted for the modernization of Orderly Bazaar slaughter house.

Pune Gets A Brand New Slaughterhouse, To Be Leased Out

Abhijit Atre, Times News Network, May 17, 2005

The UP state government has done some deal with slaughter house owners and is issuing new licences due to which the population of livestock in the state has come down drastically. Cows are being illegally slaughtered.

Though slaughtering of cow is banned and the animal is worshipped by Hindus, the menace of cow slaughtering has increased in the present regime. As a result of this, the population of cattle and livestock has come down drastically in Uttar Pradesh. (PTI)

~ Hriday Narain Dixit, BJP spokesperson and MLC, May 2, 2011

The recently modernised slaughter house at Kondhwa will be handed over to a private agency on a built operate and transfer (BOT) basis. According to the administration, the Pune Municipal Corporation (PMC) has spent around Rs. 4 crore on modernisation of the slaughter house which stands on a PMC owned land, cost of which is Rs. 3 crore.

The expenses on modernisation were met from the grants issued by the state and the central government. The PMC operates the slaughter house between 4 am to 9 am. After the five hour use the slaughter house is kept unused.

The private agency has shown willingness to operate the slaughter house on a commercial basis by paying an annual rent of Rs 66 lakh to the PMC, provided the agency is allowed to run the slaughter house from 4 am till 10 pm.

Gurgaon And Faridabad: Soon, Wait For High-Tech Slaughterhouse May End

HT Correspondent, Hindustan Times Gurgaon, February 16, 2013

Government is moving fast in the direction of setting up two high-tech slaughterhouses at Gurgaon and Faridabad at the cost of Rs. 60 crore and Rs. 56 crore respectively. The municipal corporations of Gurgaon and Faridabad have submitted a proposal in 2011.

Now for the first time in a kingdom well protected by the arms of the kings of the Kuru dynasty, I see you grieving with tears in your eyes. Up till now no one on earth has ever shed tears because of royal negligence.

The protection of the lives of both the human beings and the animals is the first and foremost duty of a government. A government must not discriminate in such principles. It is simply horrible for a pure-hearted soul to see organized animal-killing by the state in this age of Kali. Maharaja Pariksit was lamenting for the tears in the eyes of the bull, and he was astonished to see such an unprecedented thing in his good kingdom. Men and animals were equally protected as far as life was concerned. That is the way in God's kingdom.

~ Srila Prabhuapda (Srimad Bhagavatam 1.17.8)

Naresh Kadian, a member of a committee set up by the government on slaughterhouses, said illegal slaughtering has been taking place in Gurgaon. According to him, these slaughterhouses were flouting rules framed for prevention of cruelty to animals. The member asked civic agencies to implement the norms effectively.

5 New Mechanized Slaughterhouses Proposed For Bhubaneswar

Times News Network, Apr 18, 2013

Bhubaneswar Municipal Corporation (BMC) has engaged a Kerala-based consultancy to prepare a detailed project report (DPR) of five proposed mechanized slaughterhouses in the city. But the projects are moving at snail's pace, causing resentment among meat vendors.

The proposed modern slaughterhouses at Pandara, Gadakana, Dumduma, Ghatikia and Vani Vihar were supposed to be commissioned in 2012. Though the city has two slaughterhouses at Meherpalli in Laxmisagar area and Gandamunda, they are lying defunct.

The state government has already allotted land for each slaughterhouse. Around Rs.15 crore would be spent for the construction of five slaughterhouses. The state government and Union ministry of food processing industries would equally share the amount. Sources said the Centre was initially insisting for one big slaughterhouse for the entire city. However, the BMC sought several abattoirs to cater to the need of people at different locations.

Therefore I say that today the leaders are all fourth-class men. And that is why the whole world is in a chaotic condition. We require learned spiritual teachers -- first-class men-to lead. If people will take Bhagavad-gita's advice, then everything will be all right. What is the use of fourth-class men leading a confused and chaotic society?

If I speak so frankly, people will be very angry. But basically, their leaders are all fourth class. First-class men are great devotees of the Lord, who can guide the administrators and the citizens through their words and practical example.

~ Srila Prabhupada (JSD 6.5: Slaughterhouse Civilization)

Ludhiana - Slaughterhouse In For A Major Upgrade

Nidhi Singhi, Times News Network, Apr 25, 2010

Following strict directions from Punjab and Haryana High Court, the municipal corporation has shortlisted three companies to upgrade the slaughter house situated at Hambran Road.

Authorities have asked the firms to submit their financial bids so that work could begin soon.

Talking to Times Of India, municipal commissioner A K Sinha said four companies had approached them for the job and after going through their presentations, three were shortlisted. "The bids will be submitted soon, following which tenders will be allotted to the company on BOT basis," he added. He said the work would take at least three months to complete.

Aurangabad Slaughterhouse May Go Hi-Tech

Niraj Chinchkhede, Times News Network, Dec 8, 2012

A German company which specialises in modern slaughter and meat processing systems has evinced interest in developing the city's slaughter house at Padegaon.

The representatives of the company, BANSS Germany, who visited the Aurangabad Municipal Corporation (AMC), gave a

> *Then he [Maharaja Pariksit] asked the bull: Oh, who are you? Are you a bull as white as a white lotus, or are you a demigod? You have lost three of your legs and are moving on only one. Are you some demigod causing us grief in the form of a bull?*
>
> *At least up to the time of Maharaja Pariksit, no one could imagine the wretched conditions of the cow and the bull. Maharaja Pariksit, therefore, was astonished to see such a horrible scene. He inquired whether the bull was not a demigod assuming such a wretched condition to indicate the future of the cow and the bull.*
>
> *~ Srila Prabhuapda (Srimad Bhagavatam 1.17.7)*

presentation on how the slaughter house could be developed into a state-of-the-art centre with machines doing most of the work. They also presented how waste generated at the slaughter house could be managed and converted into fertilizers.

> *That depends on the person. Sometimes...Those who are pious persons, they know that these rats, they are also hungry and they should be given some food. That is the vision of the pious person. And that is stated in the Srimad-Bhagavatam, that in your house you should see not only to the welfare of your children. Even there is a lizard, there is a rat, even there is a snake, you should see how they are also comfortably situated. That is spiritual communism. In Vrndavana still, a snake found in the house is never killed, snake. Still a rat is never killed. If you kill a rat in Vrndavana, then so many people will come: "Oh, you are committing such sinful acts. You are killing a rat." That depends on the mentality of the person. You can take care of this animal, I mean to say, against the disturbance created by this animal, but you cannot kill them. That is not. But when it is unavoidable, we have to do like that. But as far as possible we should avoid. We have heard from our father that his elder brother in the village had a cloth shop, and there were rats. So at night he would keep a big bowl of rice in the middle of the shop, and the rats will eat whole night. They would not commit any harm to the cloth. They respect it. They are also hungry, they are also living entities. They have also right to live, to eat. Isavasyam idam sarvam [Iso mantra 1]. Everything. They are God's creatures. The food is not only meant for you, that you shall simply eat rice and not allow to the rats and cats. No. That is not Vedic injunction. You will find in the Srimad-Bhagavatam. You can take precaution. After all, they are animals. But you cannot kill.*
>
> *Of course, that is Western philosophy, that because the animals are increasing, they should be killed. We Indians also, we have taken that view—because we cannot give protection to the cows, they must be sent to the slaughterhouse. That is the modern view. But that is not injunction of the Vedas. The Vedas says that everyone has right to live, every living entity. That is going on not only in consideration of the animals—even in human beings. Just like the Americans, they were all Europeans, and they entered this American land, killed so many Red Indians. So these kind of things are going on, but that does not mean that is the law. You killed so many Red Indians for your benefit, but you have to suffer for that.*
>
> *~ Srila Prabhupada (Lecture, Surat, India, 1970)*

The proposed project would cost Rs 33.68 crore, with the central government offering a 50 per cent subsidy. The corporation will have to make arrangements for remaining funding. Highly placed sources in the civic body said it would adopt a public private partnership (PPP) model or a build, operate and transfer (BOT) option to give shape to the project.

The slaughter house at Padegaon will be spread over 36 acres area.

BANSS Germany supplies modern slaughter and meat processing systems as well as storage and cooling room transport systems for cows, pigs and sheep.

Emu Slaughterhouse To Come Up On Hubli Outskirts

Vincent D'Souza, Times News Network, Sep 3, 2011

An emu slaughter house -- where the birds will be slaughtered and their meat processed is taking shape on the outskirts of the city. Indo-Aussie Emu Farm, which is installing the project at Sulla village at a cost of Rs 2 crore has plans to export the meat.

The installation works of the slaughter house and two cold storage units having a storage capacity of two tonnes each will be completed by December end. The slaughtering machine has been imported from Germany. The farm which has helped around 60 farmers take up emu farming in several parts of the state by providing chicks will buy back the grown up birds from them.

Farm proprietor Vinny John said he has got advance orders mainly from Iraq, Iran, Mecca and Goa. The meat which will be exported to Muslim countries will be of purely Halal standard, he added.

According to Vinny John, who is currently doing a research on emu breeding in University of Western Australia, the Australian origin bird was first brought to India by an American NRI about 10 years ago who set up a farm in Andhra Pradesh. Then it spread

> *Starvation, world hunger, cruelty, waste, wars -- we must make a statement against these things. Vegetarianism is my statement. And I think it's a strong one.*
> - Isaac Bashevis Singer, Nobel laureate and Holocaust survivor

to Maharasthra, Tamil Nadu, Karnataka and northern states. The promoters of emu rearing have been regularly organizing food festivals in metros where emu dishes are served for people to develop a taste for the red meat.

Nagpur To Get A 'Scientific' Slaughterhouse

Times News Network, Jul 27, 2011

The Nagpur Municipal Corporation (NMC) will be constructing an ultra-modern slaughter house on the city outskirts. NMC has dropped its earlier plan to upgrade its old abattoir in Bhandewadi.

Sukrut Nirman Charitable Trust, a social organization working for protection and welfare of animals, has filed a plea claiming that majority of slaughterhouses are running illegally as they haven't sought permission of Maharashtra Pollution Control Board (MPCB) and Animal Welfare Board of India before opening as per rules of Prevention of Cruelty to Animals Act, 1960.

For Slaughterhouse, Chandigarh MC To Cough Up Rs 15cr

Deepak Yadav, Times News Network, Feb 19, 2012

There is fresh hope for city residents to get hygienic meat on their plate. After previous attempt to run a temporary slaughter house failed, MC has finally decided to cough up Rs 15 crore for automatic poultry processing plant in the financial budget for 2012-2013 and approached national meat and poultry processing board of ministry of food processing to provide consultancy on this project.

A senior official of the MC said, "We are in touch with the national meat and poultry processing board to provide consultancy

---

We simply request, "Don't kill. Don't maintain slaughterhouses." That is very sinful. It brings down very severe karmic reactions upon society. Stop these slaughterhouses. We don't say, "Stop eating meat." You can eat meat, but don't take it from the slaughterhouse, by killing. Simply wait, and you'll get the carcasses.

After all, how long will the cows live? Their maximum age is twenty years, and there are many cows who live only eighteen, sixteen, or ten years. So wait that much time; then regularly get dead cows and eat. What is the difficulty?

~Srila Prabhupada (JSD 6.5: Slaughterhouse Civilization)

to us to establish plant and following this board has recently sent their consultancy proposal along with their terms and conditions to us. We will soon visit some of the private giants to establish the plant with latest and environment friendly technology."

Pig Slaughterhouse in Allahabad, The City Of Kumbha Mela

Times News Network, May 26, 2009

The Allahabad Municipal Corporation (AMC) has failed to open a pig slaughterhouse outside the municipal limits of the city though plans for it were finalized long ago.

Even the money sanctioned by the Central government for the construction of the slaughter house is lying unutilised for the last three years. The Central government has sanctioned Rs 26.16 lakh for the purpose. The AMC had to arrange the remaining 50 per cent of the amount from its resources. However, the severe financial crisis grappling the corporation has put brakes on the project.

The land for the construction of the slaughterhouse has been identified at Naini and boundary wall has been constructed. The remaining work had to be stopped due to lack of funds. The AMC officers are hopeful that if amount of Rs 15 lakh is arranged, then the project could see the light of the day.

Pimpri Chinchwad Municipal Corporation Plans Abattoir In Industrial Area

Siddharth Gaikwad, Times News Network Aug 18, 2012

After hunting for a suitable spot for an abattoir for the past many years, the Pimpri Chinchwad Municipal Corporation (PCMC) has proposed to construct a modern abattoir in an industrial area. The civic body's previous proposals for abattoir at various sites had faced opposition in the past for their inconvenient location.

> *This killing of animals is for the non-civilized society. They cannot... They do not know how to grow food. They were killing animals. When man is advanced in his knowledge and education, why they should kill? Especially here, we see so many nice foodstuffs. Fruits, grains, milk. And from milk, you can get hundreds of nice preparations, all nutritious.*
> *-Prabhupada (Room Conversation, July 5, 1975, Chicago)*

At present, Pimpri-Chinchwad has only one small slaughter house located below the Indira Gandhi Railway Over Bridge (ROB). Traders sell meat from rows of shops that the PCMC has constructed under the bridge.

The municipal corporation has now proposed to construct the slaughter house on a hectare of land in survey number 202 at Pimpri Waghire.

The proposed slaughter house will have all modern facilities, including proper disposal of the waste.

Kolkata Municipal Corporation In A Hurry To Build Abattoir

Times News Network, Jan 7, 2011

A year has passed since the Centre sent a Rs15 crore grant to build a modern slaughter house in Tangra, but KMC has not even invited a tender. The money is bound to be returned if nothing is done by end of this fiscal.

Now, in the eleventh hour, MMiC health, Atin Ghosh is on a frantic effort to at least begin the project. Mayor Sovan Chatterjee on Thursday laid the foundation stone of the slaughterhouse, next to the old one, and assured that it would be one of the most modern abattoirs in the country. A KMC source said the new slaughter house will cost Rs 29 crore and be ready by 2012.

Ghosh promised that the meat processed in the slaughter house will be disinfected and pass hygiene tests at a lab to be built in the

Therefore, according to Vedic scripture, those animal-eaters, they should kill them personally so that they can see how much suffering is there, so he will stop. But now the things are being done in the slaughterhouse. They do not see. They purchase very nicely packed. They do not know. And they are becoming implicated. Therefore, according to Vedic injunction, if you want to eat meat, you kill yourself in your front,
~ Srila Prabhupada, (Morning Walk -- June 29, 1974, Melbourne)

facility. The meat will be transported in refrigerated vans. It will also accommodate more animals.

The existing abattoir can hold 700 big animals a day, but the new one can hold 2,000 and process 80-90 animals per hour.

Delhi Goverment Constructs Hi-tech Abattoir, Lands In Trouble

Dhananjay Mahapatra, Times News Network, Mar 5, 2009

The ultra-modern abattoir built at Ghazipur at a cost of Rs 123 crore does not even conform to a 1939 British Raj scheme for a slaughter house at Najafgarh, alleged the apex pollution control board in the Supreme Court on Wednesday.

This startling allegation made by Central Pollution Control Board counsel Vijay Panjwani before a Bench comprising Justices S B Sinha, V S Sirpurkar and Cyriac Joseph startled the

---

The personality of religious principles, Dharma, was wandering about in the form of a bull. And he met the personality of earth in the form of a cow who appeared to grieve like a mother who had lost her child. She had tears in her eyes, and the beauty of her body was lost.

The bull is the emblem of the moral principle, and the cow is the representative of the earth. When the bull and the cow are in a joyful mood, it is to be understood that the people of the world are also in a joyful mood. The reason is that the bull helps production of grains in the agricultural field, and the cow delivers milk, the miracle of aggregate food values. The human society, therefore, maintains these two important animals very carefully so that they can wander everywhere in cheerfulness. But at the present moment in this age of Kali both the bull and the cow are now being slaughtered and eaten up as foodstuff by a class of men who do not know the brahminical culture. The bull and the cow can be protected for the good of all human society simply by the spreading of brahminical culture as the topmost perfection of all cultural affairs. By advancement of such culture, the morale of society is properly maintained, and so peace and prosperity are also attained without extraneous effort. When brahminical culture deteriorates, the cow and bull are mistreated, and the resultant actions are prominent by the following symptoms.

~ Srila Prabhuapda (Srimad Bhagavatam 1.16.19)

---

court. Absence of an approach road to the abattoir results in the transporting vehicles whipping up dust clouds, which would defeat the purpose -- supply of hygienic meat to Delhiites.

While stressing that there was no environment management plan prepared by MCD and the Delhi government for the abattoir, CPCB detailed the February 6, 1939 plan prepared by then Delhi Municipal Committee for setting up an abattoir at Najafgarh spread over 277.3 acres with every possible amenity, many of which were not provided for at the Ghazipur slaughter house.

The Ghazipur slaughter house got mired in controversy from 2004 onwards when MCD abruptly decided to increase the animal handling capacity of the abattoir from 2,500 per day to 5,000 without the upward revision of the earlier estimated project cost of Rs 65 crore.

While only 2,500 animals are slaughtered at Idgah, nearly 10,000 would be slaughtered at Ghazipur.

State's First Modern Slaughterhouse On The Cards For Indore

Bagish Jha, Times News Network Mar 18, 2012

Indore Municipal Corporation (IMC) is all set to develop the first of its kind state-of-the-art slaughterhouse in Madhya Pradesh with a zero waste disposal facility. Though the civic body is yet to identify the place for the slaughterhouse, it is likely to come up on eight acres of land on the outskirts of the city at an estimated cost of Rs 50 crore.

A proposal for a similar slaughterhouse for Bhopal is also in the pipeline.

---

tatas canu-dinam dharmah
satyam saucam ksama daya
kalena balina rajan
nanksyaty ayur balam smrtih
Sukadeva Gosvami said: Then, O King, religion, truthfulness, cleanliness, tolerance, mercy, duration of life, physical strength and memory will all diminish day by day because of the powerful influence of the age of Kali.
~Srila Prabhupada (SB 12.2.1)

The slaughterhouse will be developed on public-private partnership (PPP) basis under which 15% of the cost will be borne by the Union government and the remaining 85% will be shared by the company, which will be picked through tender. The IMC has to allot land for the slaughterhouse.

"The state-of-art slaughterhouse will be operated on a zero waste disposal basis," said the zoo in-charge Dr Uttam Yadav, who is supervising the project, adding that the waste from the slaughterhouse would be disposed scientifically. Other features of the slaughter house include a collection centre, main slaughtering and chilling chambers, storage room, packaging and processing centres. "It will also have provision for a market to sell and purchase animals," said Yadav adding most of the metros have such modern slaughterhouses and soon Indore will join the league.

Interestingly, there are three authorized slaughterhouses in the city at Sadar Bazaar, Khajaran and Junni Adda. But sources said that there 35 unauthorized slaughterhouses operating in the city.

The consumption of meat in Indore is about 500 kg everyday. The proposed slaughterhouse will have the capacity to produce more than the existing demand. The company, which will develop the slaughterhouse, will also export meat from here.

Dutch Know-how For Hyderabad Slaughterhouse, Completion Delayed

Times News Network, Aug 24, 2012

Mayor Mohammed Majid Hussain along with GHMC officials visited Ramanaspura slaughter house on Thursday and took up the issue of delay in completion of modernisation works with the contractor. He asked the contractor to complete work and conduct a trial run in October.

> *There are four classes: lazy intelligent, busy intelligent, lazy foolish, and active foolish. The active foolish is a fourth-class man. So at the present moment they're very active, but they're all foolish. Therefore the world is in danger. Active foolishness. Foolish, if he stops, he does not work, it is better. But as soon as he becomes active he becomes more dangerous.*
>
> *-Srila Prabhupada (Lecture, , Los Angeles, December 8, 1973)*

Upgradation and modernisation of Ramanaspura slaughter house was handed over to Ramky Enviro Engineers Ltd in 2009. The works were slated to be completed within two years but was delayed. The mayor also informed that technical experts from Netherlands will arrive in Hyderabad in September to install equipment at the slaughterhouse.

Thiruvananthapuram Slaughterhouse To Get A Lease Of Life

Aswin J Kumar, Times News Network, Dec 3, 2012

The corporation-run slaughter house in Kunnukuzhy is likely to get a fresh lease of life following the civic body submitting a fresh proposal to install a rendering plant.

The slaughter house has been facing closure following a pollution control board notice.

The corporation, in its bid to save the unit, had earlier planned to set up a rendering plant to process the waste. The government, however, denied administrative sanction, citing technical hurdles in allotting the necessary funds.

While rejecting the plan, the government had also directed the corporation to submit a fresh proposal.

It was in this backdrop that the corporation submitted the fresh proposal.

Practically there is no mercifulness now, daya. Formerly a man was very charitable, but here, at the present moment, where is the question of charity? He cannot maintain oneself. So these things are reducing. Therefore Vyasadeva thought it wise to give the Vedic knowledge in writings so that we can read, we can hear, and we can utilize, we can take benefit out of it.

-Srila Prabhupada (Sunday Feast Lecture — Los Angeles, January 19, 1969)

The corporation had earlier drawn a detailed project proposal to convert the rendering plant into a major marketing venture. According to that project, the rendering plant was to be set up at a cost of Rs 2 crore, and was to function on a build, operate and transfer basis.

The byproducts from the rendering plant like tallow, (a hard, fatty substance made from rendered animal fat), grease and MBM (meat and bone meals) were to be marketed by a private agency, which would also operate the plant.

Deonar Slaughterhouse, Mumbai

This abattoir is located in Deonar, in the eastern suburb of Mumbai. The abattoir is the largest in Asia. At present it kills 4000 animals daily and employs a workforce of 1200 butchers. 50% of its production is exported to Gulf countries and it uses 1.7 million liters of water everyday. Animals are brought from Gujarat, Rajasthan, MP, Maharashtra and UP.

Run by Municipal Corporation of Greater Mumbai, its operating losses run into crores which are borne by the taxpayers.

Plans have been finalized for a Rs.125 crore makeover of the slaughterhouse to process 14000 animals everyday. Members of public and some lawmakers are opposing the plans.

"I do not want my tax money to fund the death of any more animals," says Yogesh Shah, a Jain who runs the Mumbai-based Himsa Virodhak Sangh, or anti-violence association.

State Run Slaughterhouses

By this, he refers to a law dating back about 130 years, when the British made slaughterhouses a government responsibility, and municipal corporations began running the abattoirs across India. Over the last 60 years, slaughterhouses have increased more than 100-fold, from 345 to about 36,000, and the cattle population has declined by 1.18% a year.

"Now, they want to expand the Deonar slaughterhouse and increase its killing capacity from 4,000 to 14,000 animals," says Shah. He explains that law requires the state to provide meat only for the local population. A Bombay Municipal Corporation resolution of 1983 prohibits the state from exporting "any meat, beef or pork whatsoever from this country".

But, Deonar slaughterhouse records reveal that it has exported the meat of bullocks, goats and sheep. Records show that meat of 387,953 cows and buffaloes and 10,878,424 sheep and goats was illegally exported to West Asian countries between 1990 and 2006. Allegations of financial mismanagement have also dogged the slaughterhouse and records of the same period reveal that the abattoir has made losses to the tune of Rs. 89 crore.

Others such as the municipal corporator Manoj Kotak, question the presence of the state in the meat business. "Just regulate the slaughterhouses and provide them to private, licensed operators. Why should a municipality run them? And if it is doing this for the non-vegetarian citizens, then it should run a vegetable house for the vegetarians, too. Why does it not start that enterprise as well?"

He declares that his party will oppose any move to expand the abattoir. "We will not let it happen. There is no need to kill cattle in India to export them to other countries. Certainly, no need for the state to do it."

4.

Pink Revolution

A Historic Policy Shift, Unprecedented In India's History

India is known all over the world as a peace loving country. It is a historical fact that India never attacked any other country, believing always in the philosophy of peaceful coexistence.

It is also probably the only country that provides for animal care in its constitution. Animals are mentioned as something more than just food. Each citizen is enjoined to care for and preserve nature and its creatures.

Article 48, The Directive Principles of State Policy states, "The state shall, in particular, take steps for ... prohibiting the slaughter of cows and calves and other milch and draught cattle."

India has been a country of farmers and shepherds, lovingly looking after their animals. India was never a country of butchers and murderers. Bloodbath is foreign to Indian culture.

Compassion and non-violence formed the core belief of all the religions that originated in this great land.

Traditional Indian or Vedic way of life teaches respect for all life forms. In their view, all living beings are born of mother nature and

And the rascal, blind leaders are leading everyone to hell. They are simply misleaders. People do not like to accept any authority. Still, they have accepted these rascals as leaders and are being misled. In this way both the rascal leaders and their unfortunate followers remain bound up by the stringent laws of material nature.
~Srila Prabhupada (Beyond the Limits of the Body)

have an equal right to life. Indeed, in Vedic conception, animals are treated like innocent children and are meant to be given all protection.

Srimad Bhagavatam, the foremost of all Vedic texts states, "One should treat animals such as deer, camels, asses, monkeys, mice, snakes, birds and flies exactly like one's own son. How little difference there actually is between children and these innocent animals." (SB 7.14.9)

National Policy Takes A U-turn

10 years ago it marked a significant moment in Indian history when Indian government decided to accord highest priority to meat consumption and export, making it 'truly a national initiative'. Website of Ministry of Food Processing Industries states:

> There is an urgent need to frame a right strategy for the development of meat and poultry production in the country. This will certainly bring prosperity to millions of our rural citizens and create employment in rural India. Having achieved the Green Revolution, the White Revolution and the Blue Revolution, it is time to ask the question "can the Pink Revolution be far behind?" Certainly this will require large investment in infrastructure, mainly in cold storages, and modern meat processing plants. Without a strong and dependable cold chain, a vital sector like meat industry, which is based mostly on perishable products, cannot survive and grow.
>
> (http://mofpi.nic.in/ContentPage.aspx?CategoryId=173)

These so-called civilized people -- what is the difference between these rascals and vultures? The vultures also enjoy killing and then eating the dead body. "Make it dead and then enjoy" -- people have become vultures. And their civilization is a vulture civilization. Animal-eaters -- they're like jackals, vultures, dogs. Flesh is not proper food for human beings. Here in the Vedic culture is civilized food, human food: milk, fruit, vegetables, nuts, grains. Let them learn it. Uncivilized rogues, vultures, raksasas [demons] -- and they're leaders.
~ Srila Prabhupada (Journey of Self Discover 6.5: Slaughterhouse Civilization)

Also, below we reproduce excerpts from the report of the working group on food processing industries for 12th five year plan by Government of India.

Ministry of Food Processing Industries
Excerpts From Report of the Working Group on Food Processing Industries For 12th Five Year Plan, Government of India

11th Plan (2007-2012)

The total plan outlay of the Ministry rose from 650 crore during the 10th Plan to 4,031 crore during the 11th Plan.

The financial projections for the 12th Plan have to be looked at from the perspective of making growth of food processing sector truly a national goal and reflect both the potential of the sector and demand from the stakeholders.

Likely Impact

The proposed financial outlay of around 15,300 crore would have an aggregate component of around 10,300 crore towards providing part capital assistance to food processing projects. Based on design of the Schemes and experience so far, this may be able to attract a total investment

The foolish leaders of a godless civilization try to devise various plans to bring about peace and prosperity in the godless world under a patent trademark of materialism, and because such attempts are illusory only, the people elect incompetent, blind leaders, one after another, who are incapable of offering solutions. If we want at all to end this anomaly of a godless civilization, we must follow the principles of revealed scriptures like the Srimad-Bhagavatam and follow the instruction of a person like Sri Sukadeva Gosvami who has no attraction for material gain.
~ Srila Prabhupada (Srimad Bhagavatam 2.2.6)

of around 35,000 crore in food processing sector. Considering an Incremental Capital Output ratio of around 4 for Indian Economy, though it may be less for food processing sector, an additional investment of 35,000 crore may lead to an additional output of 8,750 crore.

The Mid-Term Appraisal Report of the 11th Five Year Plan has also recommended accelerating agricultural growth through high value segment (horticulture, livestock and fisheries). To achieve this, it has suggested, inter-alia, the following:

---

nijagrahaujasa virah
kalim digvijaye kvacit
nrpa-linga-dharam sudram
ghnantam go-mithunam pada
Once, when Maharaja Pariksit was on his way to conquer the world, he saw the master of Kali-yuga, who was lower than a sudra, disguised as a king and hurting the legs of a cow and bull. The King at once caught hold of him to deal sufficient punishment.

The king cannot tolerate insults to the most important animal, the cow...Human civilization means to advance the cause of brahminical culture, and to maintain it, cow protection is essential. There is a miracle in milk, for it contains all the necessary vitamins to sustain human physiological conditions for higher achievements. Brahminical culture can advance only when man is educated to develop the quality of goodness, and for this there is a prime necessity of food prepared with milk, fruits and grains. Maharaja Pariksit was astonished to see that a black sudra, dressed like a ruler, was mistreating a cow, the most important animal in human society.

The age of Kali means mismanagement and quarrel. And the root cause of all mismanagement and quarrel is that worthless men with the modes of lower-class men, who have no higher ambition in life, come to the helm of the state management. Such men at the post of a king are sure to first hurt the cow and the brahminical culture, thereby pushing all society towards hell. Maharaja Pariksit, trained as he was, got the scent of this root cause of all quarrel in the world. Thus he wanted to stop it in the very beginning.
~ Srila Prabhuapda (Srimad Bhagavatam 1.16.4)

---

i. To encourage "clustering" of farmers in groups through NGOs, be it in the form of "cooperatives", farmer clubs, or contract farming, etc.

ii. To encourage organized logistics players, processors and modern retailers (both domestic and foreign) by freeing them from restrictions, and supporting them to link directly with clusters of farmers.

This is a matter of great satisfaction for the Ministry of Food Processing Industries that the above suggestions have already been the guiding principles of its 11th Five Year Plan.

The Scheme for Modernization of Abattoirs was the third important component of the Infrastructure Development Scheme of the Ministry. This Scheme aimed at creating infrastructure for hygienic and more humane slaughtering of animals leading to availability of hygienic meat to the domestic consumers as well as exports. This Scheme also has requisite flexibility for spirit of Public-Private Partnership and has generated good response from the States.

The 11th Plan approach of the Ministry also gave special stress on creation of institutional structures to guide the growth of the sector in the desired direction. The establishment of National Meat and Poultry Processing Board and Indian Grape Processing Board

---

Saunaka Rsi inquired: Why did Maharaja Pariksit simply punish him, since he was the lowest of the sudras, having dressed as a king and having struck a cow on the leg?

Saunaka and the rsis were astonished to hear that the pious Maharaja Pariksit simply punished the culprit and did not kill him. This suggests that a pious king like Maharaja Pariksit should have at once killed an offender who wanted to cheat the public by dressing like a king and at the same time daring to insult the purest of the animals, a cow. The rsis in those days, however, could not even imagine that in the advanced days of the age of Kali the lowest of the sudras will be elected as administrators and will open organized slaughterhouses for killing cows.

~ Srila Prabhuapda (Srimad Bhagavatam 1.16.5)

may be considered as significant milestones during this period. The Indian Institute of Crop Processing Technology was also upgraded to a National Centre of Excellence in the country. Above all, a National Institute of Food Technology Entrepreneurship & Management (NIFTEM) has been established by the Ministry as a Centre of Excellence to cater to all aspects of technology, entrepreneurship, research, skill development and management for the sector at the apex level.

Various studies suggest that the industry is grappling with the shortage of refrigeration mechanics, electricians and fitters and food safety professionals etc. There are a few institutions only that provide qualified manpower for food processing sector. Hence, one of the major emphasis of 12th Plan would be on mapping the skill gaps and identify priority areas for human resource development for increasing the productivity of workers/units in the sector.

iii. Scheme for Cold Chain, Value Addition and Preservation Infrastructure

Capital grant of 50% / 75% of the project cost (plant and machinery and technical civil work only) in general areas/difficult areas subject to a maximum of 10 crore.

Cold chain network in India is practically non-existent with stand alone cold storage facilities passing of as cold chain network. Most of the cold stores are single chambered, single product facilities which mainly stock potato and potato seed for about 6 months a year and lie idle during the rest of the year. The entrepreneurs, setting up cold chain projects, have to grapple with the procurement issues as well which lead to low capacity utilization.

People in general are misled by blind leaders. The leaders of human society -- the politicians, philosophers and scientists -- are blind because they are not God conscious. According to Bhagavad-gita, because they are bereft of all factual knowledge due to their atheistic way of life, they are actually sinful rascals and are the lowest among men.

When such atheists become leaders of society, the entire atmosphere is surcharged with nescience.

~ Srila Prabhupada (Nectar of Instruction: verse 7)

The Ministry of Food Processing Industries has been fully aware of the need for comprehensive cold chain solutions for food processors. The Scheme for Integrated Cold Chain, Value Addition and Preservation Infrastructure was therefore launched during 11th Plan to provide integrated cold chain and preservation facilities without any break, from the farm gate to the consumer.

The Scheme is designed to link farms to value addition facilities through an efficient supply chain and includes sectors such as dairy, meat, poultry and fishery too in addition to fruits and vegetables

Out of 164 proposals, 39 cold chain projects have been approved initially which met all eligibility parameters within stipulated timeline. The approved proposals envisage a total investment of about 850 Crore which would be creating an additional aggregate cold chain capacity of about 2.5 lakh MT in the Country. Most of these projects are under implementation and a significant part of them may be completed by end of this year.

Considering very encouraging response from industry, the Ministry has decided to cover more cold chain projects under the Scheme during 11th Plan and has already received in principle approval from the Planning Commission in this regard.

It is being proposed to support 120 more integrated cold chain projects during 12th Plan, out of which 20 projects would be of irradiation facilities.

iv. Scheme for Modernization of Abattoirs

Capital grant of 50% / 75% of the project cost (Plant machinery and technical, civil work only) in general areas/difficult areas subject to a maximum of 15 crore.

Value addition in meat sector has been almost non-existent except in the case of cattle meat processing which is primarily meant

It is a grossest type of sin to eat meat supplied by organized slaughterhouses which are ghastly places for breeding all kinds of material afflictions to society, country and the people in general. The material world is itself a place always full of anxieties, and by encouraging animal slaughter the whole atmosphere becomes polluted more and more by war, pestilence, famine and many other unwanted calamities.
~ Srila Prabhupada (Srimad Bhagavatam 1.7.37)

for the export market. *Livestock markets and abattoirs are mostly in unorganised sector. For the meat sector to be more vibrant, profitable, export oriented and provider of safe meat, it is necessary that a perceptible shift from unorganized to organized sector takes place.*

Mid-Term Appraisal of 11th Five Year Plan

The rise in per capita income in the Country has witnessed an increased demand for meat products in recent years. It is to be noted that meat consumption remains a "luxury" for majority of non-vegetarian population in India. However, as the purchasing

---

O chaste one, the king's good name, duration of life and good rebirth vanish when all kinds of living beings are terrified by miscreants in his kingdom. It is certainly the prime duty of the king to subdue first the sufferings of those who suffer. Therefore I must kill this most wretched man because he is violent against other living beings.

When there is some disturbance caused by wild animals in a village or town, the police or others take action to kill them. Similarly, it is the duty of the government to kill at once all bad social elements such as thieves, dacoits and murderers. The same punishment is also due to animal-killers because the animals of the state are also the praja. Praja means one who has taken birth in the state, and this includes both men and animals. Any living being who takes birth in a state has the primary right to live under the protection of the king. The jungle animals are also subject to the king, and they also have a right to live. So what to speak of domestic animals like the cows and bulls.

By the law of the Supreme Lord, all living beings, in whatever shape they may be, are the sons of the Lord, and no one has any right to kill another animal, unless it is so ordered by the codes of natural law. The tiger can kill a lower animal for his subsistence, but a man cannot kill an animal for his subsistence. That is the law of God, who has created the law that a living being subsists by eating another living being. Thus the vegetarians are also living by eating other living beings. Therefore, the law is that one should live only by eating specific living beings, as ordained by the law of God. The Isopanisad directs that one should live by the direction of the Lord and not at one's sweet will. A man can subsist on varieties of grains, fruits and milk ordained by God, and there is no need of animal food, save and except in particular cases.

~ Srila Prabhupada (Srimad Bhagavatam 1.17.10-11)

---

power of the people rise, there has been a perceptible shift towards meat and poultry consumption, which is also being reflected in food inflation figures. The poultry industry has though risen to this challenge and a number of organized players have entered this segment to take optimum advantage of this increasing demand. But the domestic supply chain of the poultry sector also leaves much to be desired.

Unfortunately, the meat sector remains unorganized except cattle meat processing for export market. This has led to not only continuous upward pressure on meat prices, but also increasing concerns regarding hygiene standards of meat products. Quality and hygiene levels in the meat market continue to be major issues due to unscientific breeding, primitive and crude slaughtering and de-feathering techniques, lack of basic infrastructure facilities including facilities for handling carcass/flaying, cross–contamination in slaughter and improper handling during carriage and transportation. These issues lead to high wastages of meat, contamination and deterioration in quality during the whole process. *It was thus felt that both qualitative as well as quantitative capacities of abattoirs need to be upgraded and they are required to be appropriately linked with commercial processing of meat, both for domestic consumption and export markets besides discouraging unauthorized slaughtering.*

Creation of the infrastructure of Meat Testing Laboratories also needs to be looked at.

In view of the above, during 11th Plan, the Ministry had launched a comprehensive Scheme for Modernization of Abattoirs across the Country. The Scheme is mainly aimed at promoting scientific and hygienic slaughtering of animals, by-product utilization and value addition, provision of chilling facility to prevent microbial activity in slaughtered animals and better forward linkage facilities for finished meat and meat products.

If man does not allow the animals peaceful coexistence, how can he expect peaceful existence in human society? The blind leaders must therefore understand the laws of the Supreme Being and then try to rule.
~ Srila Prabhupada (Srimad Bhagavatam 1.13.47)

The Scheme is to be implemented with the involvement of local bodies (Panchayats and Municipal Corporations) and also has the flexibility for facilitating involvement of private investors through competitive bidding. Professional agencies are also being involved by the Ministry for project appraisals, implementation and monitoring of projects.

A. Status Of Implementation

As in the case of Mega Food Parks and Integrated Cold Chain projects, the Ministry initially decided to take up 10 abattoir projects in the first phase. The approved 10 projects are under various stages of implementation in Dimapur (Nagaland), Kolkata (West Bengal), Ranchi (Jharkhand), Shimla (Himachal Pradesh), Hyderabad (Andhra Pradesh), Patna (Bihar), Ahmednagar (Maharashtra), Jammu (Jammu & Kashmir), Srinagar (Jammu & Kashmir) and Shillong (Meghalaya). Two of these projects viz. Dimapur and Ahmednagar have been completed and commissioned. The third project at Hyderabad is likely to be completed by December, 2011.

---

etam drstim avastabhya
nastatmano 'lpa-buddhayah
prabhavanty ugra-karmanah
ksayaya jagato 'hitah

Following such conclusions, the demoniac, who are lost to themselves and who have no intelligence, engage in unbeneficial, horrible works meant to destroy the world.

The demoniac are engaged in activities that will lead the world to destruction. The Lord states here that they are less intelligent. The materialists, who have no concept of God, think that they are advancing. But according to Bhagavad-gita, they are unintelligent and devoid of all sense. They try to enjoy this material world to the utmost limit and therefore always engage in inventing something for sense gratification. Such materialistic inventions are considered to be advancement of human civilization, but the result is that people grow more and more violent and more and more cruel, cruel to animals and cruel to other human beings. They have no idea how to behave toward one another. Animal killing is very prominent amongst demoniac people.
~ Srila Prabhuapda (Bhagavad-gita 16.9)

Other projects have also received requisite approvals, including environmental clearance, and are under construction.

Major challenges of the Scheme remain identification and acquisition of land and complex regulatory issues related to such projects. Considering the challenges of the sector, though, the progress of the Scheme may be considered satisfactory.

B. Recommendations For 12th Plan

In view of the satisfactory progress and further interest shown by various State Governments, the Sub-group report has recommended continuation and further upscaling of this Scheme.

It is proposed to establish 90 new abattoirs and modernize 150 existing abattoirs during 12th Plan. It is also being recommended that while these projects may remain owned by municipal bodies, the responsibility of Operation and Management (O&M) of these facilities may be ideally done by private sector, appointed through a transparent bidding process.

Finally, this Scheme is recommended to become part of the proposed NMFP (National Mission on Food Processing) to be implemented by State Governments since most of the proposals are from the Municipal Bodies who are closely connected to the State Governments.

However, as the system of approval of abattoir projects at the State level, as a component of NMFP (National Mission on Food Processing), may take some time to come into operation, it is

The cow is not my mother? Who can live without milk? And who has not taken cow's milk? Immediately, in the morning, you require milk. And the animal, she's supplying milk, she's not mother? What is the sense? Mother-killing civilization. And they want to be happy. And periodically there is great war and wholesale massacre, reaction.
-Srila Prabhupada (Garden Conversation, June 14, 1976, Detroit)

proposed that the Scheme for Modernisation of Abattoir may continue to be operated as Central Sector Scheme by the Ministry till 31 March 2014. *It is envisaged that under Central Sector Scheme, during first two years of the 12th Plan, 40 abattoir projects would be take up which would include 20 projects for setting up new abattoirs and 20 others for modenisation of existing abattoirs.* In addition, the Ministry would continue to be directly responsible for remaining grant to be given to projects sanctioned during the 11th Plan.

During 11th Plan, the Ministry has already provided assistance to around 2,000 units under this Scheme with around similar number of units likely to be assisted with proposed enhancement in budget allocation.

Scheme For Supporting Cold Chain Facilities For Non-Horticultural Produces And Reefer Vehicles

At present, NHM/NHB programmes provide funding support for standalone modern cold storage facilities horticultural produces. However, such support is not available for nonhorticultural projects dealing with dairy, fish, poultry, meat etc.

It is proposed to support such projects now under NMFP (National Mission on Food Processing) with the same funding pattern as available under the Central Sector Scheme supporting integrated cold chains, i.e., capital grant of 50% and 75% of the project cost for general areas and difficult areas respectively. This initiative would also support projects for acquisition of reefer vehicles for efficient transportation of food processing products.

> *Pariksit Maharaja was an ideal king and householder because he was a devotee of the Personality of Godhead. And the Emperor was a typical example of this. Personally he had no attachment for all the worldly opulences in his possession. But since he was king for the all-around welfare of his citizens, he was always busy in the welfare work of the public, not only for this life, but also for the next. He would not allow slaughterhouses or killing of cows. He was not a foolish and partial administrator who would arrange for the protection of one living being and allow another to be killed. Because he was a devotee of the Lord, he knew perfectly well how to conduct his administration for everyone's happiness -- men, animals, plants and all living creatures.*
> *~ Srila Prabhupada (Srimad Bhagavatam 1.4.12)*

C. Scheme For Modernization Of Meat Shops

This Scheme has been designed to address increasing concern about public health arising out of contamination and poor quality of meat being made available from meat shops in urban areas. It is believed that small investments by these meat shops in basic infrastructure (e.g. tiles, SS wash basin, exhaust and ventilation systems) and equipment (cutting table with SS base, deep freezer, sealing machine etc.) would go a long way in promoting hygienic meat consumption and thus give further fillip to this sector.

Each meat shop is proposed to be provided with maximum grant of 3 lakh, depending on eligible items, through this Scheme which may be implemented as part of NMFP through local urban bodies. *It is proposed to modernize 10,000 meat shops during the 12th Plan in the Country.*

D. Scheme For Human Resource Development (HRD)

All the activities being conducted by the Ministry under this Scheme would be now made partly available to the State Governments through NMFP. In case of Skill Development for the food processing sector, which is a gigantic task, the same would be implemented through NIFTEM (National Institute of Food Technology Entrepreneurship and Management) which

"These blind leaders, they do not know." They are especially mentioned, andha yathandhair upaniyamanah. The leaders, they lead others. So, yad yad acarati srestha tat tad evetaro janah [Bg. 3.21]. Leaders are responsible because yad yad acarati srestha: "Those who are leaders, whatever they do, they perform, common men follow that." Therefore they must be very perfect. Common men follow the leaders. If the leaders are themselves imperfect, then what will be the position of the common men?

So here it is said that because the leaders, they do not know what is the aim of life, what is the goal of life, therefore common men, people in general, they are being misguided. They are being misguided. Suppose a blind man leads some other blind men. What will be the result? Both of them will meet danger.

~ Srila Prabhupada (Srimad-Bhagavatam 7.5.31 -- Mauritius, October 4, 1975)

would work as the apex body to plan strategic roll out, implement and monitor this development of around 3 million skilled people for the food processing sector during next 7–8 years. This would be achieved by networking with the existing Government/non-Governmental/private organizations as well as establishing some new structures wherever required.

The Ministry would handle/coordinate all the work pertaining to skill development till such time NIFTEM becomes fully operational and capable enough to handle the skill development as envisaged in the foregoing. The Ministry would continue to give the overall policy framework and monitor progress achieved by NIFTEM in this direction.

I. Creation Of Infrastructure Facilities For Running Degree/Diploma/Certificate Courses In Food Processing Technology

This is to encourage introduction of specialized courses in food processing technology in recognized Colleges/Educational Institutions. Apart from Degree/Diploma courses, certain short duration Certificate courses may also be considered under the Scheme. These courses may be of duration of 3–6 months and initiated preferably through Industrial Training Institutes/Polytechnics. The level of assistance available for creation of requisite infrastructure is proposed to be enhanced from existing 75 lakh to 1 crore for each proposal.

II. Entrepreneurship Development Programme (EDP)

This is to promote entrepreneurship in food processing sector. Eligible institutions may be provided assistance of 2 lakh per EDP during 12th Plan. The Curriculums for such programmes may be standardized with the assistance of NIFTEM to keep them abreast of developments in the food processing industry and till such time the existing curriculum would be continued.

III. Food Processing Training Centre (FPTC)

These Centres are basically meant for development of rural entrepreneurship and transfer of technology for processing of food products by utilising locally grown raw material and providing hands-on experience at such production–cum-training centres. Thus, these Centres would be helpful in promoting entrepreneurship/skill development as well as transfer of technology

The entire outlay for HRD activities during the 12th Plan would now be implemented under NMFP though the Ministry would be directly releasing remaining assistance for projects sanctioned during 11th Plan, for which 6 crore each for next two years has been provided.

E. Scheme For Promotional Activities

Out of the total proposed budget for various promotional Schemes of the Ministry, 50% of funds would be made available to State Governments through Mission during 12th Plan. Some of

> *Has this civilization produced anything but quarreling individually and nationally? Has this civilization enhanced the cause of equality and fraternity by sending thousands of men into a hellish factory and the warfields at the whims of a particular man? It is said here that the cows used to moisten the pasturing land with milk because their milk bags were fatty and the animals were joyful. Do they not require, therefore, proper protection for a joyful life by being fed with a sufficient quantity of grass in the field? Why should men kill cows for their selfish purposes? Why should men not be satisfied with grains, fruits and milk, which, combined together, can produce hundreds and thousands of palatable dishes. Why are there slaughterhouses all over the world to kill innocent animals? Maharaja Pariksit, grandson of Maharaja Yudhisthira, while touring his vast kingdom, saw a black man attempting to kill a cow. The King at once arrested the butcher and chastised him sufficiently. Should not a king or an executive head protect the lives of the poor animals who are unable to defend themselves? Is this humanity? Are not the animals of a country citizens also? Then why are they allowed to be butchered in organized slaughterhouses? Are these the signs of equality and fraternity and nonviolence? Therefore, in contrast with the modern, advanced, civilized form of government, an autocracy like Maharaja Yudhisthira's is by far superior to so-called democracy in which animals are killed and a man less than an animal is allowed to cast votes for another less than animal man.*
>
> *~ Srila Prabhupada (Room Conversations -- July 26, 1975, Laguna Beach)*

the promotional activities to be funded under Mission would be as follows:

i. Organizing seminar/Workshops

For organizing seminars/workshops, State agencies and industry associations would be eligible for grant up to 50% of the cost, subject to a maximum of 7 lakh per event.

ii. Conducting studies/survey

For conducting studies/surveys or preparation of feasibility reports etc., agencies would be eligible for grant up to 50% of the cost, subject to a maximum of 10 lakh for each proposal.

iii. Support to exhibitions/fairs

In case of financial assistance to any institution/organization for organizing a fair/exhibition or sponsoring/co-sponsoring of a fair/exhibition, quantum of assistance may be decided on merits of the proposal by State Mission, subject to a maximum assistance of 7 lakh.

iv. Advertising And Publicity

Killing is illegal, according to the law of God. But the government does not want to follow God's law. They would rather follow their own cruel whims.

On the one side, the government prohibits the flesh-eaters from eating animals who have died a natural death. On the other side, they allow the flesh-eaters to put millions of animals to most unnatural, painful death in slaughterhouses.

These rascals are in power. But legally -- according to God's law -- they should permit flesh-eaters to eat only animals who have died a natural death.

In India, for example, after some animal has died, people come and take the carcass away -- free. They get it without any cost to themselves. They get the skin for making shoes and so forth. They get the flesh for eating. Let them cook and eat it if they want. The farmer does not charge anything. Why slaughterhouses? Take this."

So some day, when the government is made up of godly men, there will be no more slaughterhouses. And you'll be able to advertise, "Here is a cow carcass -- available free." Those who are butchers and tanners can take the flesh and skins free.

~ Srila Prabhupada (Morning walk, New Orleans)

The proposed activities under the Mission would need to be given adequate publicity to ensure their optimal utilisation. This would be more critical during initial years. Thus, there would be provision for funds for dissemination of information and creation of necessary awareness about various Schemes to be covered under the Mission.

National Meat And Poultry Processing Board (NMPPB)

National Meat and Poultry Processing Board (NMPPB) is another much needed institution for a sector, which is mostly unorganized and has remained neglected, due to both historical and cultural reasons. *The Ministry is though fully seized of the huge potential of this sector in coming years and has therefore mandated NMPPB to guide the sector through its future growth path.* The Board would have focus on evolving and adherence to modern standards of hygiene and quality in this sector, through initiatives for standardization, testing etc. The activities that are proposed for NMPPB during the 12th Plan include:

i. Studies/Surveys/Research

ii. Outreach Activities

iii. Training programs for butchers, municipal officials and entrepreneurs

iv. Establishment expenses of NMPPB

v. Promotional activities like participating in exhibitions, seminars etc in India and abroad

vi. Filling patterns

> *When we kill the animals to eat them, they end up killing us because their flesh, which contains cholesterol and saturated fat, was never intended for human beings.*
>
> *~Williams C. Roberts, M.D., editor of The American Journal of Cardiology*

vii. Establishing food testing Laboratories

Indian Grape Processing Board (IGBP)

The growth potential of wine sector necessitated creation of Indian Grape Processing Board (IGPB). This Board, located at Pune amidst grape growing area, would be aiming at making Indian wine a preferred product in both domestic and foreign markets. For this purpose, IGPB is creating a detailed Action Plan with special stress on increasing efficiency and quality upgradation.

Academic Programs

The National Meat And Poultry Processing Board (NMPPB) began offering formal degree courses at bachelors, masters and doctoral levels in food process engineering from 2009-10 academic year. In B.Tech program 40 students are admitted every year, 10 students in the M. Tech program and 5 in the Ph.D programs.

In a significant related decision, based on recommendations of the concerned Sub-group report, it is proposed to bifurcate the NMPPB and create separate Boards for meat and poultry. The necessary steps would be taken soon and suitable provisions would be made in the 12th Plan for expanding their activities. *Thus, the existing NMPPB would be converted into a Board looking after meat processing only. This is being proposed as it has been felt that both meat and poultry sectors are sufficiently large, with their own special needs and separate sets of stakeholders, to warrant dedicated Boards.*

It is further proposed to set up a National Meat Processing Training Centre and 20 Meat Quality Labs in the Country to ensure all round development of this sector.

People everywhere are suffering on account of being led by blind leaders who are devoid of all knowledge of the soul. Such foolish men lead other foolish men and all concerned suffer. Andha yathandhair upaniyamana, when one blind man leads another, the result is that both of them fall into the ditch. Therefore there is a requirement for a section of society to become first-class men, free of the influence of the modes of material nature, who can understand the mission of this human form of life and who can teach it to others.
~ *Srila Prabhupada (A Transcendental Diary, Vol.4)*

Promoting Innovations

The need for innovation has never been felt more as India strives to find a delicate balance between growth aspirations of its poor and increasing concerns about environmental degradation.

The decision to declare 2010–2020 as a "Decade of Innovation" and setting up of National Innovation Council (NIC) may be regarded as significant steps in this direction. In keeping with this national goal, the Ministry has decided to make innovation in food processing, part of its central theme of planning for the 12th Plan.

As mentioned in the previous sections of this Report, dealing with strengthening of institutions and promotion of R&D, the establishment of NIFTEM (National Institute of Food Technology Entrepreneurship and Management) is part of this belief to encourage product and process innovations in food processing sector. Further, the existing Schemes as well as proposed measures for promoting R&D efforts are also expected to promote innovation. It is though felt that encouraging innovations may require much more efforts and thus it is now proposed to introduce some direct measures for this purpose.

Summary Of Financial Projections For 12th Five Year Plan (2012-17)

There is a total financial projection of 15,304 crore for the 12th Five Year Plan. More than 75% of this is accounted for by Infrastructure Development Scheme and National Mission on Food Processing. Further, out of around 11,750 crore under these two initiatives, an amount of 10,300 crore has been proposed towards part capital support to projects like Mega Food Parks, Integrated

---

mrgostra-khara-markakhu-
sarisrp khaga-maksikah
atmanah putravat pasyet
tair esam antaram kiyat
One should treat animals such as deer, camels, asses, monkeys, mice, snakes, birds and flies exactly like one's own son. How little difference there actually is between children and these innocent animals.
(Srimad Bhagavatam 7.14.9)

Cold Chains, modernization of abattoirs and setting up of other food processing units.

The total financial outlay of around 15,300 crore would have an aggregate component of around 10,300 crore towards providing capital assistance to projects such as food parks, cold chains, abattoirs, on-farm infrastructure and other food processing units.

As has been mentioned earlier, the Ministry would be targeting skill development of 3 million persons under its proposed skill development programme. This programme would thus prepare rural youth for working with food processing industry and ensure that the sector, with above projected investment and growth, does not face any manpower issues.

5.

Subsidies And Tax Rebates

On Meat Processing And Export

Taxes on processed food in India are among the highest in the world. No other country imposes excise duty on processed food.

No country distinguishes between branded and unbranded food sectors for taxation. There is excise duty of 16% in the form of CENVAT levied on food products and then there is sales tax, octroi, mandi samiti, entry tax and customs duty on material, levied by the Central/State/Local bodies. The net effect ranges from 21% to 30% on various food items. India is the only country to have levied excise duty on machinery and equipment for processed foods. Indian consumers are very price-sensitive and cost reductions are imperative to raise demand and consumption of food products. Since the net effect of various taxes falls directly on the price, the off-take of processed food items remains low. Consider the Food and Vegetable sector, where against the installed capacity of 21 lakh tonnes (of the units registered under FPO), present production is only 9.4 lakh tonnes or about 45%.

But all these tax strictures apply only to the non-meat products. When it comes to meat products, it's a different ball game altogether. In fact, meat is the most subsidized commodity and meat sector is the most pampered sector in the entire Indian economy.

Everything related to meat - raising animals, their slaughter, transportation, retail outlets, pre-cooling facilities, cold storage, brand publicity, quality control, packaging development, brand publicity, export and even shipping is subsidized by the government.

Ignoring millions of children who die of malnutrition every year, the central government is spending thousands of crores to subsidize an industry which only serves vested interests - mostly underworld mafia and big agribusinesses. Meat is being made increasingly available to few meat eaters in the country while the prices of vegetables, grains and milk are doubling every year.

Some excerpts from the website of the Ministry of Food Processing Industries:

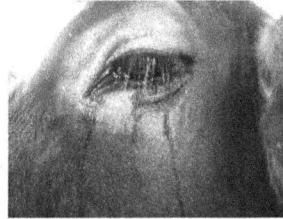

There are no restrictions on exports of poultry and poultry products. The government provides some transportation subsidies (Rs 3-15 per kg) for its exports. There are a number of issues that need to be addressed to fructify and ensure the growth for the current markets, industry sources expressed.

For the development of meat export from India the industry has demanded some immediate measures like financial assistance for upgradation of export oriented abattoirs/processing plants, inclusion of cattle meat under APEDA's Transport Assistance Scheme for new markets in Africa/CIS where freight cost from India for reefer containers is much higher than from competing countries, restoration of DEPB rates for frozen cattle meat, exemption from Service Tax on transportation of meat products processed for exports.

(http://mofpi.nic.in/ContentPage.aspx?CategoryId=173)

Below is an article which sheds further light on the subject. It was published in Times of India on August 10, 2012.

'Withdraw Subsidies To Meat Exporters'

Times News Network, Aug 10, 2012

The Central government has been urged to abolish subsidies to meat trade and exports which is not only taking toll on productive

---

Cow protection is our life. Krsna has ordered, 'krsi-go-raksya.' Cow protection at any cost. It is Krsna's order. We have to execute it. Any government allowing slaughterhouses should be removed, but we are not so powerful.
~ Srila Prabhupada TKG's Diary: July 13

cattle but is also creating shortage of milk. "There is an immediate need to arrest the present practice of indiscriminate slaughter of young and productive animals. Otherwise, the problem will intensify and the country will have to face acute shortage of milk," said Kanakrai Savadia, managing trustee of Sukrut Nirman Charitable Trust, an organization working to save cows in Vidarbha.

In a memorandum submitted to Anand Sharma, the union minister of commerce and industry, Savadia has said the prevailing high prices of bovine, milk and meat are strong indication of

The next symptom of the age of Kali is the distressed condition of the cow. Milking the cow means drawing the principles of religion in a liquid form. The great rsis and munis would live only on milk. Srila Sukadeva Gosvami would go to a householder while he was milking a cow, and he would simply take a little quantity of it for subsistence. Even fifty years ago, no one would deprive a sadhu of a quart or two of milk, and every householder would give milk like water. For a Sanatanist (a follower of Vedic principles) it is the duty of every householder to have cows and bulls as household paraphernalia, not only for drinking milk, but also for deriving religious principles. The Sanatanist worships cows on religious principles and respects brahmanas. The cow's milk is required for the sacrificial fire, and by performing sacrifices the householder can be happy. The cow's calf not only is beautiful to look at, but also gives satisfaction to the cow, and so she delivers as much milk as possible. But in the Kali-yuga, the calves are separated from the cows as early as possible for purposes which may not be mentioned in these pages of Srimad-Bhagavatam. The cow stands with tears in her eyes, the sudra milkman draws milk from the cow artificially, and when there is no milk the cow is sent to be slaughtered. These greatly sinful acts are responsible for all the troubles in present society. People do not know what they are doing in the name of economic development. The influence of Kali will keep them in the darkness of ignorance. Despite all endeavors for peace and prosperity, they must try to see the cows and the bulls happy in all respects. Foolish people do not know how one earns happiness by making the cows and bulls happy, but it is a fact by the law of nature. Let us take it from the authority of Srimad-Bhagavatam and adopt the principles for the total happiness of humanity.

~ Srila Prabhuapda (Srimad Bhagavatam 1.17.3)

shortage of supply. Even existing slaughterhouses are not able to meet requirements. Hence, they are procuring buffaloes by illegal means.

The most unfortunate fallout of this has been the deleterious effect on small farmers. They are lured to sell their animals, but soon discover that it is impossible to buy fresh stock again. The slaughterhouses involved in export are killing productive cattle clandestinely to fulfil their export commitments.

Savadia said in India farmers mainly rear cattle for agriculture purpose as well as milk production. When the animal grows old and is not fit for either milk production or agricultural purpose, it is sold at throwaway prices to the traders involved in meat export. Thus the traders get animals at an extremely low cost. To fulfil the demand these animals are even stolen and slaughtered.

In abattoirs even milk-giving animals are slaughtered illegally to meet the export demand of traders. He pointed out that slaughterhouses maintained and run by local bodies are meant for domestic requirement of meat and not export. Yet, these establishments are involved in illegal export of meat.

Savadia said despite violations subsidies are offered by the Central and state governments for construction and upgradation of slaughterhouses and the prevailing meat trade in the country.

At the present, especially on this planet earth, the influence of Lord Brahma has decreased considerably, and the representatives of Hiranyakasipu—the Raksasas and demons—have taken charge. Therefore there is no protection of brahminical culture and cows, which are the basic prerequisites for all kinds of good fortune. This age is very dangerous because society is being managed by demons and Raksasas.
~ Srila Prabhupada (Srimad Bhagavatam 7.3.13)

He said the Agriculture Agricultural and Processed Food Products Export Development Authority (APEDA) is providing 25% to 60% subsidy on transport of meat, pre-cooling facilities, cold storage, brand publicity, quality control, packaging development, brand publicity etc.

In addition, there is exemption from sales tax and income tax. The modern export-oriented slaughterhouses are mostly run by private players who earn huge profits at the cost of our water bodies and environment, causing pollution and diseases.

Savadia urged Sharma to withdraw all the subsidies offered to meat trade. "The subsidy of thousands of crores of rupees from taxpayers' money is not justifiable from any angle," he added.

Centre Slammed Over Subsidy for Beef Exports

October 28, 2012, Outlook

Gujarat chief minister Narendra Modi today reiterated the charge that the Centre was promoting beef exports by providing subsidies even while levying duty on cotton exports.

Speaking at the 4th Annual General Meeting of the Jain International Trade Organisation here, Modi said "The UPA government allows subsidy to open slaughterhouses, whereas cotton farmers are levied duty for exporting cotton".

He alleged that to facilitate mutton exports, tax is waived off for five years. "The union government does not want another green revolution and white revolution, but wants to promote pink revolution," Modi alleged, adding that he had to approach the Supreme Court to get a law enacted to ban cow slaughter in his state.

He said that it is possible to bring change within the system if motives are noble, intentions are clear and policies are coherent.

Vegetarians have the best diet. They have the lowest rates of coronary disease of any group in the country... they have a fraction of our heart attack rate and they have only 40 percent of our cancer rate. On the average, they outlive other people by about six years now."
~William Castelli, M.D.,
Director, Framingham Heart Study, the longest-running epidemiological study in medical history.

6.

Rail Minister Signs Order

To Resume Cow Carriage Trains

Cancelling an earlier order of the previous government, in September 2004, railway minister Laloo Prasad Yadav permitted the transport of cattle on trains all over the country. The previous government had banned the transport of cattle in 2001.

Railway Ministry officials said the transport of cows, buffaloes and goats would be subject to strict rules like certificates from district authorities and local vets.

Attacking Railway Minister Lalu Prasad for lifting the ban on ferrying of cattle by trains, the BJP alleged he was behaving as a "trader of cows for slaughter" and asked Prime to intervene to stop it.

BJP Vice President and spokesman Mukhtar Abbas Naqvi told reporters that the previous NDA government had put a ban on

---

An uncivilized man can do anything for the satisfaction of his senses. He can kill children, he can kill cows, he can kill old men; he has no mercy for anyone. According to the Vedic civilization, cows, women, children, old men and saintly persons should be excused if they are at fault. But asuras, uncivilized men, do not care about that. At the present moment, the killing of cows and the killing of children is going on unrestrictedly, and therefore this civilization is not at all human, and those who are conducting this condemned civilization are uncivilized demons.

~ Srila Prabhupada (Srimad Bhagavatam 10.3.22)

ferrying of cattle by train in 2002 considering that these are being transported to Bangladesh for slaughter.

"It is a matter of concern that Prasad is trying to give legal sanctity to trafficking of cows for slaughter," he alleged, asserting that his party will oppose it.

Sources said after a series of representations from various bodies, including confidential reports from the RPF and an internal audit report, former Railway Minister Nitish Kumar had imposed a virtual ban on movement of cows via trains. Provisions in the existing laws were made stringent so that it was practically impossible to ferry cows by trains.

Member of Parliament and former union minister, Ms Menaka Gandhi's outburst was widely reported in the press. Following is a press report on the issue.

Railway Minister Took 'Bribe' From Cattle Mafia, Says Maneka

Tribune News Service, New Delhi, September 17

Senior leader and former Central Minister Maneka Gandhi today accused Railway Minister Laloo Prasad Yadav of taking

Unfortunately, our modern materialistic civilization is filled with so-called leaders who are devoid of spiritual knowledge and who refuse to take guidance from genuine spiritual authorities. Such leaders are blind in the truest sense, and therefore both they and their blind followers waste their time in a hopeless, meaningless struggle to be happy by gratifying the senses of the temporary material body. In defiance of God's laws for spiritual life in harmony with the laws of nature, such leaders encourage all sorts of sinful activities, such as gambling, intoxication, meat eating, and illicit sex. As a result they make civilization hellish, and in their next lives both they and their followers are thrown into hellish planets. Such leaders should certainly be known as demons. ~ Srila Prabhuapda (Back To Godhead, 12-07, 1977)

'bribe' for lifting the ban on transport of cattle in railway bogies. "One of the first order that Mr Yadav passed after assuming the charge of the Railway Minister was allowing the transport of cattle in railway bogies. It, in practical terms, means extending support to the cattle mafia that takes these animals to Bangladesh for slaughtering," she said.

The illegal cattle trade is more lucrative and bigger than drug trade, she said.

Giving details of the illegal trade, she said, "The mafia has an organisation called Howrah Cattle Dealer Association in Howrah. It runs the illegal trade by bringing lakhs of cows, buffaloes, bullocks and bulls from northern states like Punjab, Haryana to West Bengal where these animals are slaughtered or smuggled to Bangladesh."

"Bangladesh has thin cattle population of its own, but its exports of beef runs into lakhs of tonnes," she asserted to buttress her claim of smuggling of cattle to Bangladesh.

Suta Gosvami said: After reaching that place, Maharaja Pariksit observed that a lower-caste sudra, dressed like a king, was beating a cow and a bull with a club, as if they had no owner.

The principal sign of the age of Kali is that lower-caste sudras, i.e., men without brahminical culture and spiritual initiation, will be dressed like administrators or kings, and the principal business of such non-ksatriya rulers will be to kill the innocent animals, especially the cows and the bulls, who shall be unprotected by their masters, the bona fide vaisyas, the mercantile community. In the Bhagavad-gita (18.44), it is said that the vaisyas are meant to deal in agriculture, cow protection and trade. In the age of Kali, the degraded vaisyas, the mercantile men, are engaged in supplying cows to slaughterhouses. The ksatriyas are meant to protect the citizens of the state, whereas the vaisyas are meant to protect the cows and bulls and utilize them to produce grains and milk. The cow is meant to deliver milk, and the bull is meant to produce grains. But in the age of Kali, the sudra class of men are in the posts of administrators, and the cows and bulls, or the mothers and the fathers, unprotected by the vaisyas, are subjected to the slaughterhouses organized by the sudra administrators.

~ Srila Prabhuapda (Srimad Bhagavatam 1.17.1)

Rubbishing the claim that the Railways would earn revenue through this, she said this was not correct as a boggy carried over 300 cattle illegally instead of 10 permitted by the law. It resulted in damage to these bogies. Repair of bogies leads to massive loss of revenue to the Railways, she asserted.

Showing a photograph of the cattle being carried in a railway boggy on September 7 at the Mubarakpur railway station in Patiala district, she said 70 per cent of cattle perished during transportation and then their skin and meat were sold.

Sher Khan, the trader who was carrying the cattle to the Howrah railway station, was absconding, she said. He was part of the bigger mafia, she added.

Because every third head of cattle in Bangladesh is smuggled in from India. Many come from as far away as Haryana and Punjab. An estimated 20,000 to 25,000 animals enter Bangladesh almost everyday through West Bengal alone. While the trade is illegal on the Indian side, it becomes legal the moment the livestock enters Bangladesh.

Some estimates put the annual turnover from leather, meat and meat exports from smuggled Indian cattle in Bangladesh at over Rs 25 billion.

---

prsadhras tu manoh putro
go-palo guruna krtah
palayam asa ga yatto
ratryam virasana-vratah

Among these sons, Prsadhra, following the order of his spiritual master, was engaged as a protector of cows. He would stand all night with a sword to give the cows protection.

One who becomes virasana takes the vow to stand all night with a sword to give protection to the cows. Because Prsadhra was engaged in this way, it is to be understood that he had no dynasty. We can further understand from this vow accepted by Prsadhra how essential it is to protect the cows. Some son of a ksatriya would take this vow to protect the cows from ferocious animals, even at night. What then is to be said of sending cows to slaughterhouses? This is the most sinful activity in human society.

~ Srila Prabhupada (Srimad Bhagavatam 9.2.4)

She said that as per the Cattle Prevention Act, it was illegal to transport cattle across State borders for purposes of slaughter and allowed only in case of draught and milch cattle.

The Indian Railways, she said, has been transporting cattle from North Indian States only in the direction of West Bengal proved that these were then taken to Bangladesh for slaughter. "The fact that they are going to Bangladesh is undisputed," she said.

Since the Railway Ministry could not have done it on its own, so a clearance was taken from the Animal Welfare Board. The board, which is without a full-time chairman since June this year, issued a letter on July two saying the matter has been "reconsidered" and in view of "practical constrains", the rule was being relaxed.

The Transport of Animal Rules says: "As far as possible, cattle may be moved during the nights only. They should be off-loaded during the day and be fed, given water and rested and if in milk, milking should be carried out." Any violation was to be treated as criminal offence.

Only 12 cows were to be put in a bogey with prior permission of the Animal Welfare Board and a medical certificate from designated veterinary doctor was needed before that. The route plan was also to be submitted to the board. The Ministry of Home Affairs, in April, 2003, had directed the BSF (Border Security Force) to keep a vigil on smuggling of cows to Bangladesh.

That the order had been reversed was known on September 7 when activists of former Union Minister Maneka Gandhi's People for Animals stopped a train at the Chagger Railway station near Dera Basi in Punjab and foundthat hundreds of cows were loaded in the train in the most pitiable conditions en route to eastern India (http://www.tribuneindia.com/2004/20040918/nation.htm#1)

In another interview about the whole episode, Ms Gandhi told The Pioneer: "This is a national shame. Actions of the the Congress-led UPA and the Prime Minister, who is responsible for policy making, have from the beginning been anti-national whether it is arresting the people for hoisting the national flag or reversing the laws in existence since 1978 to allow open smuggling of cows to Bangladesh. Bangladesh is eating and exporting beef from Indian cows.

"In 2001, the Railways, after a careful study, came to a conclusion that they had somehow been abetting the crime of sending the cows to West Bengal on false certifications. It thus imposed a ban.

"The new order of the UPA Government effectively means that it was reopening the smuggling route of sending the cows to Bangladesh for slaughter."

Toppling the Congress Party coalition that had ruled India for 48 of the 49 preceding years in 1998, the Hindu nationalist Bharatiya Janata Dal coalition beefed up the Cattle Transport Act by banning cattle transport by train in March 2001, under the 1960 Prevention of Cruelty to Animals Act. The action had long been urged by then-animal welfare minister Maneka Gandhi and then-Animal Welfare Board of India chair Guman Mal Lodha as an essential step toward ending cattle slaughter, which increased 20-fold between 1977 and 1997.

And cruelty to animals means not to be cruel to the cats and dogs. And for the cows, "Oh, there is no question of cruelty. It has no soul. Kill him." This is your civilization, Dog civilization.

One side they're advertising "Stop cruelty to animals," another side they're opening unrestricted slaughterhouse. Just see. Just like a gang of thieves gives a signboard, "Goodman and Company." So there are so many members of the society against cruelty to animals. But they are all meat-eaters.

-Srila Prabhupada (Talk with Bob Cohen - February 27-29, 1972, Mayapura)

7.

White Lies

And Blatant Cover-ups

E ven in the face of the facts mentioned so far, the government maintains its stand that it is not doing anything to promote meat consumption and export. Like they say..."You can't fool all the people all the time...but you can fool enough to run a large country." Following news reports might illustrate this point better.

Narendra Modi-Sharad Pawar Squabble Over Meat Export 'Subsidy' Continues

Published: Thursday, Apr 19, 2012, Place: Anand (Gujarat) | Agency: PTI

Gujarat Chief Minister Narendra Modi on Wednesday once again raised the issue of "subsidy" on meat exports, but Union Agriculture Minister Sharad Pawar countered it saying no such concession is being given by the Central government.

Modi and Pawar were present at the unveiling of National Dairy Plan under the Mission Milk. The mission, touted as second white revolution, aims to augment the production of milk to meet its raising demand.

"I am concerned about the UPA government encouraging 'pink revolution'. By pink revolution I mean encouraging export of mutton and also subsiding it," Modi said from the dais in Anand.

Subsidising meat has also affected milk production of the country as animals get killed for their meat without any proper

Make the lie big, make it simple, keep saying it, and eventually they will believe it. ~ Unknown

curbs, he said. There is a "big racket" involving smuggling of cows to Bangladesh, he alleged and said the issue needs serious thinking.

Pawar, reacting to Modi's statement, said after the programme, "Government of India's meat export policy has not changed since the last 15 to 20 years. There has been no new amendments by the UPA government and there is no concession provided for its exports."

"I am surprised the issue was raised today by Modi who spoke of 'pink revolution'. The issue (of subsidy) has never come up before the government in the last seven years."

"I would have given answer to the issue raised by Modi on the dais itself. But I did not do it because I wanted to maintain dignity of the function which was organised by the Government of India where he (Modi) was invited as a guest. Guests can raise their concerns from the dais," Pawar said.

Earlier this month at a public meeting in Rajkot, Modi had said the UPA government was taxing cotton export while giving subsidy on meat exports.

Union Commerce Minister Anand Sharma had termed Modi's remark as "unwarranted" and bereft of facts.

'Modi's Statement On Beef Exports Inflammatory'

PTI New Delhi, August 19, 2012

Commerce and industry minister Anand Sharma has hit out at Gujarat chief minister Narendra Modi accusing him of giving

> *The great masses of the people ... will more easily fall victims to a big lie than to a small one.*
> *~Adolf Hitler*

a "political slant" by making "inflammatory" statement on beef exports.

"My attention has been drawn to your public statement regarding the meat export policy alleging that the central government is promoting slaughter of cows and export of beef, which is inaccurate, inflammatory and misleading," Sharma said in his letter to Modi.

"It is unfortunate that in spite of the factual position, you have chosen to give a political slant to Government's stand on meat export policy. Public discourse on policy matters must never be allowed to be trapped in partisan political agenda," Sharma added.

In his Janamashtami message through his blog, Modi appealed to the people to reject 'pink revolution'.

He said the UPA Government led by Congress is "promoting slaughtering of cows"

Sharma said, "You are well aware that slaughter of cows is prohibited in India in harmony with principles enshrined in our Constitution".

He said meat is largely a by-product of livestock, utilising spent animals at the end of their productive life.

"Cattle and buffaloes which account for over 60% of meat production, are primarily reared for milk and towards the end of their productive life, are utilised for meat production.

As there are many parties, Communist party, Congress party, this party, that party, so there must be one Krishna's party. Why not? Then people will be happy, if Krishna's party comes to the governmental post. Immediately there will be peace. In India, there are so many slaughterhouses. There are... It is said that ten thousand cows are being killed everyday, in the land were one cow was being attempted to be killed, immediately Maharaja Pariksit took his sword, "Who are you?" In that land, now ten thousand cows are being killed every day. So you expect peace? You expect prosperity? This is not possible. Therefore if some day Krishna's representative takes the governmental power, then he will immediately stop all these slaughterhouses, all these brothels, all these liquor houses. Then there will be peace and prosperity.

~ Srila Prabhupada (Srimad Bhagavatam 1.10.2 -- Mayapura, June 17, 1973)

"A ban on meat production or export would lead to an abnormal rise of unproductive animals which is inconsistent with sound animal husbandry practices," Sharma said.

8.

Factory Farms

Coming To India In A Big Way

The majority of the world's farm animals currently live in miserable conditions, raised using 'production line' methods. High output is achieved by subjecting the animals to intense and prolonged suffering.

They live short, barren lives, spent in cages, crates, overcrowded sheds and narrow stalls.

Exporting Factory Farms : The Global Expansion of Industrialized Meat Production

From The Food Empowerment Project

It is frightening that our species now eats more than five times more meat than we did back then in 1950. These days, over 50 billion land animals are killed for food worldwide every year - and that number is expected to double by 2030. Rising incomes in large, rapidly-developing countries are driving a major shift in global dietary patterns as those societies strive to emulate the West's eating habits.

The factory farming techniques that make the mass-production of meat, dairy and eggs possible cause incalculable harm and cruelty to animals, the environment and people—so why would these countries choose to follow this path?

The main reason is that some multinational agribusiness companies see serious profit in expanding their operations to largely untapped emerging markets. These corporations have already saturated the Western world with their products, so in order to maintain their economic superiority, companies must break into countries where consumer demand for meat and animal products is rising, environmental and animal welfare regulations are lax, and labor is enticingly cheap. Namely, established agribusiness giants are actively advancing into Asia and nations in the Global South—threatening to supplant traditional agrarian practices and wreak the very same kind of havoc they have done in the U.S.

A brief look at the past provides a chilling glimpse into the planet's potential food future. Consider the historical precedent of Tyson Foods, the world's largest meat producer, which in the late 1940s essentially invented the system of vertical integration that now serves as the model for industrialized animal agriculture. The core principle behind vertical integration is to have a single corporate entity own and control every aspect of the meat production process—from feed mills and hatcheries to slaughterhouses—so that farmers solely raise animals on contract for the company at reduced prices. This domineering system now sets the standard for the nation's chicken industry, and can increasingly be found in cow and pig production.

Six decades after its introduction, the economic efficiency of virtual integration now allows just four major companies to process over half the chickens, 80% of the cows, and 60% of the pigs consumed in the U.S. And now, this business model is enabling these same few massive corporations to expand into the consumer territories of developing societies.

We can begin to understand what this means for animals, the environment and people in other parts of the world by examining Big Ag's recent commercial activities in some of these countries.

> *The factory farm attitude is exemplified by the ISE corporation, whose lawyer asserted that it is legally acceptable to dispose of live birds as if they were manure. When the judge asked, 'Isn't there a big distinction between manure and live animals?' ISE's lawyer responded, 'No, your honour.'*

India

In 2008, Tyson also bought a majority share in Mumbai-based Godrej Foods Ltd. and expects to reap about $50 million a year in poultry sales throughout India. But the company may find that Indian society is less conducive to their vertical integration schemes than Brazil, because approximately 65% of Indians are employed in the agricultural sector, and vegetarianism is quite common. In a country where about 780 million people make a living producing food, Tyson's top-down domination strategy faces real challenges. However, meat consumption (especially chicken) is rising in India as incomes grow, and drive-through fast food franchises are spreading at an exponential rate, so company heads figure that increasing demand for meat and more convenient means of distribution will work in their favor over the long term.

Officially Stated Government Policy On Vertical integration of poultry industry : The annual per capita consumption in India is only 33 eggs and 630 grams of poultry meat. This is much lower as compared to the world average of 124 eggs and 5.9 kg meat. The National Committee on Human Nutrition in India has recommended per capita of 180 eggs (about one egg every two days) and 10.8 kg meat .To meet this target , it is estimated that by year 2010, the requirements will be 180 billion eggs and 9.1 billion kg poultry meat while the estimated production may only be around 46.2 billion eggs and 3.04 billion kg poultry meat .

The scheme has been introduced recently in few places by private sector hatcheries or feed millers. They provide chicks and feed to the producers and purchase the live broilers at a cost depending upon the body weight. Some incentives for high feed efficiency and good livability are provided. However, in most cases, the purchased birds are sold to the wholesale dealers who often dictate the price and full benefits of the scheme are not available to the farmers. The scheme needs to be supported by providing infrastructure for meat processing, packaging, preservation and marketing with value addition of products and maintaining a cold chain till the product reaches the consumer. The private sector companies including foreign investors have a great opportunity to invest in these schemes, in collaboration with the Indian entrepreneurs.

In India, both intensive and traditional systems of poultry farming are followed, but intensive system is rapidly increasing due to increasing land and other input costs. It is estimated that in India, about 60% of poultry meat and 56% of eggs are currently being produced in the intensive system. It is further estimated that there are about 60000 farms under Intensive system (some of them having more that 100000 birds) while there are about 100000 small farms scattered in rural areas practicing more extensive production systems, having flock sizes ranging from 25 to 250 birds. In case of layers the cage system is rapidly replacing the deep litter system. However in broiler farming, the deep litter system is more prevalent.

It is estimated that in year 2000, Indian Poultry Industry contribution to the GDP was about Rs 80 billion which reached to Rs. 300 billion by the Year 2005.

Lessons From China

Fast food is a $28 billion industry in China today, where there are already more than 900 McDonald's and 2,000 KFC restaurants. This is no surprise, given that China has one of the world's fastest-growing economies, with a burgeoning middle class that sees "meat" as a social status symbol signifying wealth and privilege (much like the upwardly-mobile consumers in many other developing countries). To feed this demand for animal foods, China has courted

We want to stop these killing houses. These are very, very sinful. Therefore in Europe, so many wars. Every ten years, fifteen years, there is a big war and wholesale slaughter of the whole human kind. And these rascals, they do not see it. The reaction must be there. You are killing innocent cows and animals. Nature will take revenge. Wait for that. As soon as the time is ripe, the nature will gather all these rascals, and club, slaughter them. Finished. They will fight amongst themselves, Protestant and Catholic, Russian and America, and France and Germany. This is going on. Why? This is the nature's law. Tit for tat. You have killed. Now you become killed. Amongst yourselves. They are being sent to the slaughterhouse. And here, you'll create slaughterhouse, "Dum! dum!" and killed, be killed.

~ Srila Prabhupada (Room Conversation -- June 11, 1974, Paris)

agribusiness investment from the likes of Tyson, Smithfield Foods and Novus International, and is well on its way to becoming one of the world's top meat-consuming countries. Yet, even as Chinese society increasingly emulates the Western-style diet, a legacy of ecological damage resulting from their currently unsustainable agricultural practices looms behind them, casting a dark shadow over a future that may prove even bleaker. That is, *even though factory farming is not yet the main "meat" production method in China, almost a million acres of Chinese grassland are already reduced to desert annually as a result of overgrazing and intensive farming,* and China surpassed the U.S. as the world's top emitter of greenhouse gasses in 2008. If factory farming becomes widespread in China, these problems—and many others—will become more devastating, not only to this country of 1.3 billion people, but to the rest of the world as well.

For decades, animals, people and the planet have suffered the severe consequences of factory farming as it is conducted in the Western world— and the export of this corporatized method of mass-production can only exacerbate the ethical, ecological and social problems it causes. The implications of Concentrated Animal Feeding Operations expanding across the globe are especially disturbing because most of the countries targeted by agribusinesses have even fewer animal welfare, environmental, health, and labor regulations than the U.S. or Europe, so the abuses inherent to factory farming would only worsen. Even as individuals we can make a positive difference by supporting activists in developing nations who proactively promote a diet free from animal products and work to prevent these industries from gaining a foothold in their countries.

Industrial Mega Dairy Proposal For Andhra Pradesh, Plan Opposed

P S Jayaram, 18 August 2011

The Animal Welfare Board of India (AWBI) has raised objections to the establishment of the ambitious 'Kisan' Special Economic Zone (SEZ) in Nellore district of Andhra Pradesh after environmentalists and animal lovers raised serious concerns over the proposal to set up mega dairies in collaboration with a foreign company as part of the SEZ.

According to AWBI Chairman Dr R M Kharb, the establishment of mega dairies in the coastal district involved several environmental and animal welfare risks and possible violation of rules. The AWBI is a statutory body of Government of India, working under the aegis of Ministry of Environment and Forests.

Dr Kharb, in a letter to the promoters of Kisan SEZ, raised several environmental concerns over the proposed project by a consortium of IFFCO, Fonterra, a New Zealand-based dairy company and Global Dairy Health, an Indian firm. The letter was in response to a petition by the Federation of Indian Animal Protection Organizations (FIAPO), an umbrella body of Indian animal welfare groups across the country, seeking the intervention of AWBI to stop the project.

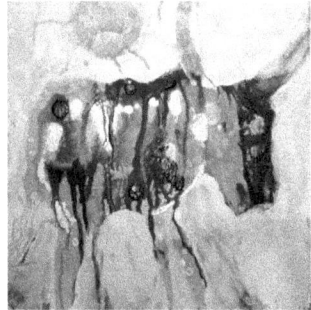

Dr Kharb said: "The proposed project is a corporate farm where animals will come under tremendous stress. The animals will be kept at high stocking densities which might result in them contracting diseases which could lead to an increased likelihood of emergence of novel zoonotic diseases."

The genetically-manipulated high-yielding cows that are proposed to be introduced in the farm have shortened life span, reduced fertility, greater propensity for diseases, physiological and development problems, environmentalists argue. "Cow slaughter and transportation for slaughter results in additional problems. The management of the amount of animal waste is also a key challenge and often results in degradation of local environment," the AWBI Chairman said. According to the convener of FIAPO, Arpan Sharma, the consortium had proposed to import 9,000 high yielding pregnant cows from New Zealand over a three year period. There were also plans to import frozen embryos and semen for subsequent breeding.

"As consumers in developed countries are demanding an end to inhumane confinement systems as is proposed in the SEZ, foreign animal production companies are looking to developing countries like India as a dumping ground for such industrial farm animal production," Sharma alleged.

"The Indian standards lag behind those of some of the developed nations with progressive animal welfare standards not being implemented by foreign companies in Indian markets. This is unfair to Indian consumers, as most of us would prefer products with high animal welfare standards," he said.

In such mega dairies, the cows are typically kept almost exclusively indoors with little or no access to natural surroundings. Cows farmed intensively like this are bred to produce unnaturally large amounts of milk which can make them more susceptible to several health problems.

Sharma pointed out that Lincolnshire in UK had recently refused permission to a cattle farm similar to the one being proposed in AP. "It is clear that the west itself is moving away from such production systems and India should not permit the establishment of such models that have demonstrated negative impacts on the environment," he contended.

A New Jungle

Meat once occupied a very different dietary place in most of the world. Beef, pork, and chicken were considered luxuries, and were eaten on special occasions or to enhance the flavor of other

> *The mlecchas, however, make plans to install slaughterhouses for killing bulls and cows along with other animals, thinking that they will prosper by increasing the number of factories and live on animal food without caring for performance of sacrifices and production of grains. But they must know that even for the animals they must produce grass and vegetables, otherwise the animals cannot live. And to produce grass for the animals, they require sufficient rains. Therefore they have to depend ultimately on the mercy of the demigods like the sun-god, Indra and Candra, and such demigods must be satisfied by performances of sacrifice (yajna).*
>
> *~ Srila Prabhupada (Srimad Bhagavatam 1.16.20)*

foods. But as agriculture became more mechanized, so did animal production. In the United States, livestock raised in the West was herded or transported east to slaughterhouses and packing mills.

Upton Sinclair's The Jungle, written almost a century ago when the United States lacked many food-safety and labor regulations, described the appalling conditions of slaughterhouses in Chicago in the early 20th century and was a shocking expose of meat production and the conditions inflicted on both animals and humans by the industry. Workers were treated much like animals themselves, forced to labor long hours for very little pay under dangerous conditions, and with no job security.

If The Jungle were written today, however, it might not be set in the American Midwest. Today, developing nations like India are becoming the centers of large-scale livestock production and processing to feed the world's growing appetite for cheap meat and other animal products. But the problems Sinclair pointed to a century ago, including hazardous working conditions, unsanitary processing methods, and environmental contamination, still exist. Many have become even worse. And as environmental regulations in the European Union and the United States become stronger, large agribusinesses are moving their animal production operations to nations with less stringent enforcement of environmental laws.

They are sending animals to the slaughterhouse, and now they'll create their own slaughterhouse. [Imitating gunfire:] Tung! Tung! Kill! Kill! You see? Just take Belfast, for example. The Roman Catholics are killing the Protestants, and the Protestants are killing the Catholics. This is nature's law. It's not necessary that you be sent to the ordinary slaughterhouse. You'll make a slaughterhouse at home. You'll kill your own child-abortion. This is nature's law. Who are these children being killed? They are these meat-eaters. They enjoyed themselves when so many animals were killed, and now they're being killed by their mothers. People do not know how nature is working. If you kill, you must be killed. If you kill the cow, who is your mother, then in some future lifetime your mother will kill you. Yes. The mother becomes the child, and the child becomes the mother.
~ *Srila Prabhupada (JSD 6.5: Slaughterhouse Civilization)*

These intensive and environmentally destructive production methods are spreading all over the globe, to Mexico, India, the former Soviet Union, and most rapidly throughout Asia. Wherever they crop up, they create a web of related food safety, animal welfare, and environmental problems.

9.

Government's Push For Livestock Business
Killing The Soul Of The Nation

According to an ANI (Asian News International) news release dated November 18th 2009, an increasing number of farmers are being motivated to undertake crop diversification and livestock farming in Punjab and other states. As part of its endeavour to ensure the growth of the livestock farming sector, the government is holding various livestock shows.

Departments of Animal Husbandry have been instructed to provide details of various government schemes to farmers. The presence of farmers at such livestock shows reflects a rapidly popularizing livestock business.

Farmers from Amritsar, Gurdaspur, Tarn Taran and Kapurthala districts recently converged in Tarn Taran to participate in the three-day "Livestock and Competition Fair".

Mahga Singh of Sarya village, who arrived here with his award winner "Goat", said: "Now, my sons have started doing this business as their family income has increased. People from all over the Punjab come to them to buy livestock." The department has registered every farmer of the area and is encouraging them to breed "Beetal Goat". They are provided with free medical aid and medicines.

There are countless such schemes to encourage farmers to give up traditional farming and take up animal rearing for meat export.

Rs. 300 Crore Scheme To Rear Male Buffaloes

Jun 29, 2009, PTI

The Centre is considering launching a Rs 300 crore scheme to rear male buffalo calves to boost meat export.

The Department of Animal Husbandry and Dairying under the Agriculture Ministry will soon approach the Cabinet for approval of the scheme, which will be funded by National Bank for Agriculture and Rural Development (NABARD).

"The proposed scheme 'Salvaging and rearing of male buffalo calves', with an estimated outlay of Rs 300 crore for the 11th Five Year Plan period, is aimed at generating employment in rural areas and earning foreign exchange for the country," a senior government official told PTI.

Under the scheme, male buffalo calves will be rescued particularly from the big cities and reared in villages, the official said, adding that this would not only lead to retaining of genetic material but also boosting buffalo meat export.

Farmers will be given incentives for rearing male buffalo calves and provided back-end linkage with export-oriented slaughter houses to buy these animals, the official said.

"There is vast potential for development of meat, by products and leather industry," the official observed.

The implementation of scheme will also lead to an additional output of buffalo meat and hides. Forex earnings will also come through export of the same.

Meat Industry - Evolving Into A Fad

Meat eaters like sexual offenders if not checked, want more and more excitement, more and more fancies to feed their fetish.

More and more Indians are trying out meats which are not supermarket staples. Illegal restaurants have sprung up selling game meat and rare birds. Our increasing interest in pushing boundaries in everything we do means that there is now a market for anything that crawls, runs, flies or swims.

One such segment being popularized is Emu meat. Farmers are selling their lands and cows to invest in emu farms, often with disastrous consequences.

India was not a meat eating or meat producing civilization. Meat eating was rare and for special occasions and confined only to a small section of our people. Today it is an industry, a fad. And that kills the soul of the nation.

India Should Ban Emu Farming

Maneka Gandhi, 07 October 2012

In 1996, an Andhra Pradesh businessman smuggled in emus through the customs, saying they were chickens from Australia. Emus look nothing like chicken but one bribe looks like another so everyone kept quiet. He multiplied these emus and started giving them to people who had poultry farms. Soon, this illegal bird spread throughout India and the animal husbandry department, who were informed again and again of the dangers of keeping this bird, jumped into its promotion enthusiastically. This Government, under Sharad Pawar (who else?) has permitted emu farming. Nabard gives loans for it.

It has spread like a disease from Andhra Pradesh to Tamil Nadu, Maharashtra, Goa, Uttarakhand and even Gujarat. It has taken 15 years and hundreds of bankruptcies to realize that emu farming is a fake – a Ponzi scheme started by clever crooks to defraud farmers. A Ponzi scheme is an investment fraud that involves the payment of so called returns to existing investors from funds contributed by new investors. Ponzi scheme organizers solicit new investors by promising to invest funds in opportunities claimed to generate high returns with little or no risk.

Let me explain to you the Great Emu Game through example:

A man called M. S. Guru started Susi Emu Farms in 2006 in Erode. He cheated 12,000 investors. It was done in two ways:

The company sold emu chicks to a farmer. The farmer was told that that once the birds were reared and adult, the company would buy them back. Many farmers turned their agricultural lands into emu rearing sheds.

Susi also asked people to invest in their emu business, paying to own emus which would be reared by Susi on a contract basis, guaranteeing Rs.1,000 per month as a return to the farmer. Many victims were lured by what appeared to be the success of Susi Farms.

Guru was conferred the Arch of Excellence (Business) Award (2008) and Gem of India Award-2011 by All India Achievers Conference.

This is what his victims have to say: "They said it was a very simple business. They promised to supply chicks and the fodder. The shed was built on my premises claiming it was free, though I had to pay a huge amount in the form of interest free security deposit," recalls P. Subrahmani from Omallaur who invested Rs. 15 lakh with Susi Farms. He got 25 others to invest. "As per the agreement, they had to pay me Rs.7,000 per month on a unit of six birds as maintenance charge. I had ten units. They made one payment and then stopped. They kept the security deposit and had no explanation for not making the payment." Those that invested in Susi directly had to give an initial investment of Rs. 2 lakh and were allocated 20 chicks. They were promised a total return of Rs. 6.5 lakh in five years.

Perunthurai, a town in Erode district is the hub of emu farming with 28 companies who have done the same thing as Susi. According to police estimates, there are over 250 promoters of contract farming of this bird across the state and they all attracted investors promising higher returns. Dozens of emu farms started operations with advertisement campaigns to lure farmers to rear the bird on contract mode in Coimbatore, Krishnagiri, Pollachi, Mettupalayam, Tirupur, Perundurai, Dharapuram and Salem . The district administration and police have now issued press statements warning people off Emu farming or investments. The Susi birds are now being fed by the government but they will all die soon as feeding them is very expensive.

> *Mam sa khadatiti mamsah. The Sanskrit word is mamsa. Mam means "me," and sa means "he." I am killing this animal; I am eating him. And in my next lifetime he'll kill me and eat me. When the animal is sacrificed, this mantra is recited into the ear of the animal -- "You are giving your life, so in your next life you will get the opportunity of becoming a human being. And I who am now killing you will become an animal, and you will kill me." So after understanding this mantra, who will be ready to kill an animal?*
> *~ Srila Prabhupada (JSD 6.5: Slaughterhouse Civilization)*

Tamil Nadu is not alone. For the last three months teams of People For Animals have been going round Uttarakhand checking emu farms. Farmers in Nainital had started breeding emus some years ago. Now, the emus have been abandoned and the farmer ruined. The farmers have stopped feeding them and lakhs of these birds are dying of starvation. Nothing can be done as there is no space to keep them.

The companies insist that the emu is a bird which is easy to keep and is very popular for its meat, oil, leather and eggs. None of these claims are true. The fact is that emu meat is a failure. It is tough and difficult to cook. In fact even Australians do not eat emu meat. Susi farms started a restaurant with emu meat as the main fare. No takers. The emus require lakhs to feed. They grow to 6 feet.

Ganesa: Some people say that in our philosophy, if we do not wish to slaughter the animals, what about the trees? We are killing the plants. They are also living entities.

Prabhupada: If you compare the animals and the trees as the same, then why not kill yourself, your brother? Why do you distinguish? Why don't you slaughter your own son? Why do you distinguish?

Ganesa: He's a relative.

Prabhupada: You discriminate. If you are slaughtering animals and you are comparing that killing of the vegetables and the killing of the animals is the same, then killing your son and killing an animal is also the same. Why do you discriminate? Just kill your own son and eat.

Paramahamsa: He's a human being, though.

Prabhupada: Ah, therefore there is discrimination. Discrimination is the better part of valor. Whom should we kill? It is all right. Jivo jivasya jivanam. But there is important. If you eat vegetables there is no crisis, you can go on. It is a fact that an animal is eating another animal. It may be vegetables or animals, but they are disturbing. Therefore it is said, "As it is allotted." You should eat such and such. Not that indiscriminately you can eat everything. If you think killing of an animal and killing a vegetable is the same, then killing of your son and killing of animals or vegetable is the same. Why do you discriminate? What is your answer?

Ganesa: So if we discriminate between the animals and the plants, well what about the discrimination between the human beings and the

(continued on next page...)

They have to be feed several times a day, 4 kg. of food each. They eat seeds, fruit, insects, young leaves, lizards, other small animals and animal droppings. They do not eat dry grasses or older leaves, even if that's all that is available to them. Emus also need charcoal to help them digest their food.

Each requires 10 litres of water daily. The female lays eggs only during October to March and the maximum number are 10-20 eggs, one every 3-5 days. Emus lay eggs with difficulty. Only a few lay eggs at one time and an incubator is needed to hatch them. But incubators are uneconomical unless there is a reasonable quantity of eggs to sustain the cost of production. They get diseases like encephalitis.

As far as selling them for food, the price of emu meat is Rs. 450 a kg – an impossible price. The egg sells for Rs. 2,200. The eggs are dark green and very difficult to eat at one go and impossible to keep. In 2010 Punjab Agro Tech promoted the emu at its business

(...continued from previous page)

animals? Is it not all right to kill animals and not human beings?

Prabhupada: No. You discriminate actually. You do not kill human beings, but you kill animals. Similarly you discriminate: instead of killing animals, kill vegetables. Importance. Just like this grass. There is enough supply of grass, but you cannot have enough supply of cows. Therefore discrimination is that it is better to live on grass than on animals. Now, still they are eating seventy-five percent other than animals. They are not eating only animals. Why not twenty-five percent more? In the market they are not eating animal. When the animal-eaters I see, they have got a little flesh, surrounded by salad and these peas and so many other things. Why don't you eat only meat?

Srutakirti: Because we require a balanced diet.

Prabhupada: No, you cannot supply. If everyone eats meat only, then one day all animals will be finished.

Paramahamsa: But we want to have a balanced diet with meat, and vegetables and fruit.

Prabhupada: That balance of diet can be done by grains and vegetables. Why should we kill animals? We know that, the balance can be done. You learn from us that balanced food can be done.

~Srila Prabhupada (Morning Walk -- May 7, 1975, Perth)

fair, saying that omelettes of its eggs were selling at Rs. 5,000 per omelette in 5 star hotels – a claim found to be utterly false. In fact, 5 stars hotels do not even have emu on their menus.

Now the emu companies are claiming that they will sell feather and nails, cooking oil and beauty products!

If the emu was being grown for meat and oil, any emu business has to have a slaughterhouse to kill the birds hygienically and another unit to process oil. No companies have these. They simply have birds which they contract out, take the money and run.

There is no meat market developed yet for export or for local sale and no symptoms of it so far. In any case there are no foreign offers for the meat. So far the oil processing and other industrial ventures remain only in newspaper and radio advertisements.

An entrepreneur in Anand, Gujarat who expected to reap huge profits from killing the bird, is now selling them away as pets. The farmers of Hoshiarpur are now bankrupt as are the emu farmers of Maharashtra – a scam that broke in 2010 and was ignored.

Uttarakhand, Maharashtra and Tamil Nadu have crashed. But that doesn't prevent more states and more ignorant state administrations from pushing emu meat. Goa, Orissa and Madhya Pradesh are pushing this. Bihar's ignorant animal husbandry and fisheries resources department minister is asking the World Bank to give Bihar money to start emu farming! His department says that they will sell it as a medicine saying that its oil has anti-inflammatory and anti-oxidative effects – a claim that even Australia does not make! Previously he had tried to make rat eating popular.

How many farmers will have to commit suicide before India bans emu farming?

They are now killing animal, but animal lives on this grass and grains. When there will be no grass, no grains, where they will get animal? They'll kill their own son and eat. That time is coming. Nature's law is that you grow your own food. But they are not interested in growing food. They are interested in manufacturing bolts and nuts.
-Srila Prabhupada (Morning Walk — June 22, 1974, Germany)

10.

Promoting Export Of Meat Will Kill Livestock-Driven Farming

Anuradha Dutt, The Pioneer, 24 May 2012

Gujarat Chief Minister Narendra Modi recently expressed concern at the Centre's 'pink revolution' — encouraging exports of meat — describing it as an anti-farmer policy. This is because livestock is diverted from farming to slaughter houses. The blame must first fall on the British, who began the practice. In fact, they changed the traditional farming system for pecuniary reasons. Under the Permanent Settlement Act, 1793, first implemented in Bengal and then in other parts, landowners were assigned fixed revenue targets by the colonial administrators and many were forced to shift to plantation farming such as cotton and indigo in place of food grains. This led to famines in the 19th century.

Cultivators were under greater pressure to meet the zamindars' demands. If the revenue target was not met, the land was auctioned off, ruining both owners and peasants. It altered India's agrarian economy, which was self-sustaining, primarily grew food grains, vegetables and fruits, reared livestock and engaged in organic farming by using animal dung, urine and manure as fertilisers, and plant and cattle derivatives as pesticides. Emphasis shifted to cash crops, and during the Green Revolution, synthetic fertilisers and pesticides. This increased the debt burden on the farmers.

Livestock-driven farming was ruined by the promotion of the meat, bones and leather industries by the British, with butchering of cattle, goat, sheep, pigs, fowls and other creatures acquiring institutional status, and mechanized slaughter houses being set up.

Later, tractors and machines further made cattle redundant among better-off farmers. The age-old ethos of compassion was completely repudiated, with free India's leaders continuing with the meat policy. Many people, overcoming food taboos and religious tenets against wanton killing, took to commerce of meat.

The constitutional directive for a countrywide ban on cow slaughter was never implemented though some States did impose a ban. A Supreme Court order in 1958, dismissing a plea by some Patna butchers that cow slaughter was a religious duty under Islam, had allowed slaughter of impotent bulls but prohibited killing of cows and calves on economic grounds. It said, "Cattle in India has three-fold uses, firstly providing milk for consumption, secondly for draught purposes; and, finally, as provider of manure for agriculture. Dung is cheaper than chemical fertilisers and extremely useful. In short, the cow and bullock are the back bone of India."

However, livestock continued to be diverted to slaughter houses to feed the thriving meat export, leather and derivatives industries. Modern India developed a culture of non-vegetarian food, sharply at variance with its pre-Raj past. Under Muslim rulers, most Hindus, barring the heterodox, shunned flesh and eggs. And cow slaughter was forbidden by many sultans out of respect for Hindu sentiments.

Emperor Akbar was said to be so very impressed by Jain tenets that he forbade killing of animals and fish, and eating of flesh for six months in a year. Foreign travellers testified to the general avoidance of flesh. JT Wheeler quoted John Fires (1678-81) on Hindu food habits in his British History under Mughal Rule, "Hindus eat fruits, vegetables, roots and rice. But they do not eat meat, fish and eggs."

In his Indian History, Part II, Wheeler quoted the late 13th century Venetian Marco Polo's Testimony, "In the entire country spreading from Cape Camorin to the Koromandal coast in the east which was earlier known as Maula Pradesh and which is the area inhabited by the Tamil speaking people; and from there the entire area up to the Bay of Bengal, which is inhabited by the Telugu speaking Telangs; no one except the Parihars (pariahs) ate beef or meat. All these people worship cows and bullocks. They do not slaughter any animal. Hence, if any traveller wishes to eat flesh of goats, he has to carry with him as servant a Syrian for doing the job of a butcher."

Much before, the Chinese Buddhist monks Fa Hien in the fifth century and Hsuang-tsang in the seventh century recorded the absence of violence against animals and consumption of flesh, or, as Fa Hien noted, even liquor.

The British made meat-eating and drinking socially acceptable. They requisitioned the services of some pliant natives. A book by Pandurang Kane, a Bombay advocate, postulated that beef was consumed in the Vedic age. Raja Rajendralal Mitra of Bengal in 1872 brought out an essay, Beef in Ancient India. He was awarded a doctorate by his masters for his effort. He later expanded this into a book, Indo-Aryan, published in 1877.

Bengal, as the seat of the Raj, provided the most fertile ground for such ideas to take root. Left-hand tantrik tradition condoned the consumption of flesh and liquor. 'Beef-eating clubs' sprouted, with English-educated natives readily breaking food taboos. If not beef, they ate other flesh and eggs and freely drank alcohol. The ethos spread throughout India as a mark of modernity.

Mohammed Ali Jinnah, Pakistan's founding father, and the Nehrus, all anglicised, relished both beef and pork. Krishna Hutheesing, Pandit Nehru's youngest sister, recalled in We Nehrus, published in 1967, "Our lunch was always of the British style and that is why we always used to have lunch in a hotel because only the British lunch included beef and pork. If beef and pork were to

India is perhaps the only nation state wherein large numbers of people subjugate their desires for the benefit of other species. That this great culture of kindness is being eroded by one of greed is very sad. I hope compassionate vegetarians of every creed are able to join hands and stop this descent into malevolence and moral turpitude. ~ Leroy Schwarz

be brought into the home, our mother and Muslim servants would have felt bad."

The genesis of the pink revolution lies in such devaluation of animal life, with unfortunate consequences for farmers.

11.

Rant To Legalize

Cattle Smuggling On Bangladesh Border

Deeptiman Tiwary, Times News Network, Dec 1, 2012

In a controversial suggestion, outgoing BSF chief U K Bansal has said that the menace of cattle smuggling on the India-Bangladesh border defies policing and might be best controlled by making the trade legal.

Cattle running mafias abound on the border, making smuggling bovines for meat a highly lucrative but violence-prone illegal business. Bansal seemed to endorse the view that the sheer scale of operations and the economic interests involved make policing a limited option.

Asked if the illegal cattle trade should be legalized given the economic realities in Bangladesh, Bansal said, "We all have to think about it seriously. It is not a problem that can be solved by policing." Bansal was speaking at BSF's annual press conference.

Several Bangladeshis lose their lives smuggling cattle for a remuneration as low as Rs 500. While trying to stop them, BSF men put their lives at risk while reports of corruption have also surfaced.

The massive demand for meat feeding a Rs 2,000 crore industry in Bangladesh has made it difficult for forces to stop the smuggling. The proposal to make cattle trade legal, despite its apparent pragmatism, is sure to attract fire from groups advocating cow protection.

Legalizing the trade is a hot potato that the government is unlikely to consider, but it could throw open a discussion on a taboo subject that might yield results later.

The issue has been contentious, leading to a stand-off between India and Bangladesh at various bilateral meets where charges have been traded. Bangladesh has rarely accepted any illegality, including the large inflow of illegal immigrants into India.

The government has made efforts to bring down casualties of Bangladeshi nationals by introducing non-lethal weapons. But the move has hurt BSF as emboldened smugglers have started attacking force personnel.

In the past three years, while casualties of Bangladeshis on the border came down by over 60%, attacks on personnel of Border Security Force went up by over 100%.

According to government figures, in 2010, as many 32 suspected intruders were shot dead by BSF on the Indo-Bangladesh border while 64 men from the force were injured due to attacks from

gam ca dharma-dugham dinam
bhrsam sudra-padahatam
vivatsam asru-vadanam
ksamam yavasam icchatim

Although the cow is beneficial because one can draw religious principles from her, she was now rendered poor and calfless. Her legs were being beaten by a sudra. There were tears in her eyes, and she was distressed and weak. She was hankering after some grass in the field.

In the age of Kali, the poor helpless animals, especially the cows, which are meant to receive all sorts of protection from the administrative heads, are killed without restriction. Thus the administrative heads under whose noses such things happen are representatives of God in name only. Such powerful administrators are rulers of the poor citizens by dress or office, but factually they are worthless, lower-class men without the cultural assets of the twice-born. No one can expect justice or equality of treatment from once-born (spiritually uncultured) lower-class men. Therefore in the age of Kali everyone is unhappy due to the maladministration of the state.

~ Srila Prabhupada (Srimad Bhagavatam 1.17.5)

smugglers. Due to continued high fatalities of its nationals, Bangladesh had been pushing for softer approach towards border guarding from India.

Thus, in 2010, India had proposed and implemented use of non-lethal weapons such as rubber bullets and pump action guns by the BSF against suspected smugglers.

Bangladeshi fatalities came down to merely 11. However, injuries to BSF men jumped to 150. In 2012, the force has recorded six deaths of Bangladeshis and 100 injuries to its men on the border.

"The problem is that the sheer economics of the trade makes it unstoppable. Close to seven lakh cattle are smuggled every year, and this is only the data collected through arrest of smugglers. The industry is worth thousands of crores of rupees in Bangladesh," said a BSF officer who has served on the Indo-Bangla border.

One of the reasons India has never been able to come to an agreement with Bangladesh on resolving the problem is the latter does not consider it smuggling, calling it cattle trade. Bangladesh has even unofficially offered to help make arrangements so that cattle can be bought at the border without risking the lives of people on either side.

You have become mad and you are engaged in doing all forbidden things which you should not do. You are doing that. And why you are doing that? Nunam pramattah kurute vikarma [SB 5.5.4]. Why? Yad indriya-pritaya aprnoti. Simply for sense gratification. Simply for sense gratification. I have seen one hotel man in Calcutta. He cut the throat of a chicken, and the chicken, half-cut, it was flapping and jumping. The child of the hotel man, he was crying, and the hotel man was laughing. He was taking pleasure, "Oh, how this chicken, half-cut throat, and how he is jumping... Why you are crying? Why you are crying?" And in Western countries I think students are sometimes taken to slaughterhouse to see. Is it a fact? Yes. You see. They take pleasure. Doing something sinful, they take pleasure. For pleasure's sake they do that.

~ Srila Prabhupada (Srimad-Bhagavatam 3.25.16 — Bombay, November 16, 1974)

12.

India-Pak Livestock Export Deal

By A.M. Parekh

India recently signed a deal with Pakistan to transfer 1 million livestock every year to Pakistan. The following is a letter from A.M. Parekh (Trustee of the Viniyog Parivar Trust) to the Prime Minister of India.

Dr. Manmohan Singh
Hon'ble Prime Minister of India,
Prime Minister's Office,
152, South Block,
New Delhi-110 011.
Respected Dr. Manmohan ji,
Re: Export of livestock to Pakistan

We understand from newspaper reports that the Government of India has permitted export of livestock from India to Pakistan. It is reported that the Pakistan administration has approved setting up of four quarantine centres immediately and another 30 to 40 over the next few months to accommodate upto ten thousand animals per quarantine centre, where the animals exported from India will be kept for 15 days before being certified as disease free and fit for slaughter for meat. The preliminary estimates of exports put the figure as 10 lakh animals per annum. Pakistan will permit duty free import of these live animals into its country.

It is also reported that this step is being taken as a measure to improve relations with Pakistan and also to increase the trade with Pakistan.

Meat is one of the 11 items which are reviewed by the Pakistan Price Control Committee and it is reported that these items are priced at 15 to 50% higher in Islamabad than in New Delhi. It is to ease the price situation in Pakistan that live animals from India will be exported.

To say the least, this is a very ill-conceived proposal. Livelihoods of a very vast number of people in rural India is dependent on rearing of animals i.e. cattle, sheep and goat. The 17th livestock census report indicates about 10% decline in population of cattle and a very negligible rise in population of sheep and goat. Even otherwise there is large scale clandestine export of livestock across the border both to Pakistan and to Bangladesh as also to the Middle East from various ports of Gujarat.

Opening up or legalizing export of livestock will be a severe blow to the Animal Husbandry in our country. It will also increase price of meat within the country. Lured by higher prices in the neighbouring country, the traders in livestock will be tempted to export more and more animals and over a period of time India will face the same situation on price front of meat that Pakistan is facing today.

We wonder whether our country has run out of ideas to improve relations with Pakistan and is considering sacrifice of dumb and innocent animals to achieve this object! Our Constitution has imposed a Fundamental Duty to show compassion towards all living beings and these duties are cast equally on the government as on the citizens. Acting against this Fundamental Duty, the

> *Just like we are taking milk from the cow. We are indebted. "No, we are killing them." They are committing simply sinful life and they want to be happy and peaceful. Just see. We are indebted. I am obliged to you for your service. So instead of feeling obligation, if I cut your throat, how gentleman I am, just see, imagine.*
>
> *~ Srila Prabhupada (Bhagavad-gita 1.37-39 -- London, July 27, 1973)*

Government has decided to export animals knowing fully well that they will be slaughtered.

Our country has adopted meat export as a Policy measure identifying it as a thrust area. This is already playing havoc with our livestock situation and a few entrepreneurs are making huge profits at the cost of our national wealth i.e. our animals. The export earnings of some three thousand crores of rupees is peanuts when compared to the foreign exchange reserve of more than 130 billion USD.

Throughout the country the public sentiment is against the export of meat which is being continued to cater to the vested interests of a few private sector entrepreneurs and their patrons in bureaucracy and politicians. It is painful to note that instead of honoring the public sentiments of banning meat export from the country the Government is taking steps now to export livestock also.

We are not elaborating on how livestock is the backbone of our rural economy as you are well aware of it.

We request you to kindly reconsider the whole issue and reverse the decision to permit export of livestock to Pakistan/Bangladesh and also to consider banning of meat export from the country.

Thanking you,

Yours faithfully, For Viniyog Parivar Trust

(A.M. Parekh) Trustee

Prabhupada: Now Kirtanananda was prosecuted because he is not killing cows.

Brahmananda: By having them grow old, they were saying that "This is cruelty. You should kill them."

Prabhupada: This is their civilization, that "You are not killing? You are cruel." Just see. Christ said, "Thou shall not kill." That is cruel. How can you pull on this civilization? But this is their religion. So what kind of persons they are?

- Srila Prabhupada (Room Conversation - February 28, 1977 Mayapur)

13.

Recognition And Awards

To Meat Exporters

In India, the meat exporter are the cynosure of all eyes. They not only receive subsidies and tax rebates, but also many awards and recognitions. Most of these exporters enjoy the coveted status of 'Star Export House'. They always seem to receive preferential treatment in selection for awards and grants.

Commonly conferred awards to them are : National Productivity Award, Rajiv Gandhi National Quality Award, National Safety Award, Industry Excellence Award, National Award For Export Excellence, APEDA Award, GMP (Good Manufacturing Practices) Award etc. Then there is a whole list of awards instituted by the Council For Leather Exports for leather exporters.

All India Meat & Livestock Exporters Association-AIMLEA claims on its home page : AIMLEA members have world class, state of the art, integrated establishments, incorporating mechanised abattoirs, operated in accordance with the Codex Alimentarius Standards, OIE Terrestrial Animal Health Code, besides having ISO 9001:2000 for Quality Systems, HACCP for Food Safety, ISO 14001 for Environment

Management and ISO 18001 for Occupational Health and Safety Management System accreditations.

India is definitely excelling in this particular area. Some of the award winning Indian meat export houses are:

- Allanasons
- Al-Noor Exports
- Al Drahim Exports Holding Private Limited
- Mirha Exports Pvt. Ltd
- Swetha Exports
- Al Safi Frozen Foods
- Abdul Majeed Qureshi & Co.
- Al Kabeer Exports Pvt. Ltd.
- Al Nafees Proteins Pvt. Ltd.
- Al Quresh Exports

Anyone who takes milk... Everyone takes milk. The cow is the mother. Mother gives milk. And mother, when she cannot supply milk, mother should be cut up. Is that a very good philosophy? Is it human philosophy? What is the answer?

You are eating everything. Except the moving cars, you are eating all the moving animals. The car also moves, but you cannot eat. Otherwise you are killing everything. You have become so civilized rascal that your business is to kill other animals and eat. You are so civilized. You are still in the crude form of human being, just like in the jungles, the aborigines, the Africans, they do not know how to develop civilization -- crude methods, eating the animals. That also, they are not so uncivilized that they keep slaughterhouses. You are so uncivilized that you are keeping slaughterhouses, regularly. These Africans and other jungle people they eat meat, but they directly kill. They have no such civilization as to maintain a slaughterhouse. The tigers eat meat, but they do not keep a slaughterhouse. And you are civilized. You are keeping slaughterhouse. Why should you keep? The government shouldn't allow you to keep slaughterhouses. If anyone wants to eat meat, let them eat like tigers and others. Individually, kill one animal -- a lower animal, not cows. This should be the government law. You kill it in your home, before your children and family, and eat. This is not good civilization.

~ Srila Prabhupada (Morning Walk -- May 10, 1975, Perth)

- Al Tamash Exports Pvt. Ltd.
- DD Marine Exports Pvt. Ltd.
- Hind Agro Industries Ltd.
- VKS Farms Pvt. Ltd.

14.

Locking Horns Over Culture And Business

Are Cattle Commodifiable Without Loss Of Traditional Farm-Life?

Sangeetha Sriram, June 2002

India has a livestock population of 500 million (20% of the world's total), more than half of which is cattle, forming the backbone of Indian agriculture. Mechanisation of agricultural operations has pushed cattle to redundancy in large parts of the country. Short hybrid grain varieties and harvester machines have reduced the availability of cattle fodder. Alongside, meat export almost doubled between 1990 and 95, while livestock population only increased by half that rate. Further, indigenous breeds of cattle have been taken over by foreign breeds introduced during the white revolution, which are treated as milch and meat machines.

From all these changes, India's cattle population is increasingly viewed as a mere economic resource for optimal returns, a transformation that is greatly impacting traditional farm-life. Recognizing this, the government instituted the National Commission on Cattle in August 2001, to suggest ways and means for the preservation and protection of the nation's cattle wealth.

But from the outset, the government's other actions have undermined the commission's work. Within the 10th five-year plan, the government has been constituting sub-committees to design policies on various sectors. Under this scheme, the sub-group on Animal Husbandry -XI - Meat Sector, constituted by the Department of Agriculture, came into being. Even as the cattle commission was drawing up policies for cattle protection, the policy recommendations of the 'meat-sector' were released;

these are clearly at odds with the commission's role and objectives. The document, in which these policy recommendations are stipulated, is peppered with phrases like "in the interest of the farmer" and "cow protection with economic spirit". The actual recommendations, however, show no such interest or spirit. Among the recommendations:

• Removal of all bans on meat export and all restrictions on processed meat import and slaughter machinery.

• Removal of all restrictions on slaughter of buffaloes.

• Reduction in the minimum age for slaughter of bullocks.

• Removal of the ban on beef exports.

The policies clearly provide a thrust towards the creation of a significant meat market supplied by industrial abbattoirs and corporate food marketeres. The main questions that arise from this are:

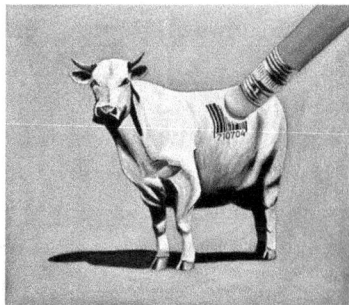

• What are the pros and cons of industrialising slaughter houses and raising more cattle for meat?

• How will these policies impact the typical Indian farmer?

• Who stands to benefit by breeding cattle for meat and expanding the meat-consumer market in India?

The answer to that last question is evident - corporations. Twenty five cattle-slaughtering factories can effectively replace all the existing 140,000 slaughter houses in the country. Next come the corporations that have built their services and products around the meat-consuming market - processors of meat into various forms of fast food, processed meat transporters, deep freezer manufacturers, cattle feed 'enhancers', drug manufacturers who sell 'meat growth

On the street, in your front, if somebody's being killed, nobody will take care; he'll go on. There is no mercifulness. Even the mother has no mercifulness, killing the child. This is Kali-yuga.

~ Srila Prabhupada (Srimad-Bhagavatam 7.6.3 -Toronto, June 19, 1976)

hormones' and antibiotics for cattle and even agri'business' banks that will give loans only for cattle 'producing'. Not to forget the fast-growing biotech industry.

Dimming Prospects In The West

An interesting phenomenon in the globalisation scene is that as the West is waking up and rejecting many harmful technologies like the use of certain chemical pesticides and waste incinerators, the private companies that have invested in them are frantically looking for markets in the less regulated, developing countries. India, with its more than one billion people, is naturally an attractive market.

Inefficient And Uneconomical Choices

The sub-group's document explains the need for India to become a livestock economy thus: "Increase in productivity of land and productivity of definite number of livestock is a necessity to meet the growing needs of human population. Thus the need for increased efficiency in livestock production and utilization is far greater today than in the past". But nothing could be farther from the truth! Vandana Shiva says in her book, Stolen Harvest "Europe's intensive livestock economy requires seven times the area of Europe in other countries for the production of cattle feed. In a complementary economy, the cattle eat the straw and agricultural waste that humans cannot. But, in a competitive model such as the livestock industry, grain is diverted from human consumption to the intensive feed for livestock. It takes eight kilograms of grain to produce one kilogram of meat."

This inefficiency - eating meat that must first be fed grain that could instead be itself eaten directly - is well known. The Meat-subgroup's proposal will move India away from her primarily complementary economy to a competitive livestock economy. By growing the cattle here for unrestricted export, India will be subsidising the meat-based industries dominated by foreign firms. By permitting them to use the natural resources in India to produce meat for export or even inefficient consumption models within India, we are creating the sort of imbalance that will divert resources away from adequate food production for our own people.

In other economic terms, too, the new policies inlcude significant dangers. A story from Stolen Harvest is instructive. "Al-Kabeer, one of the biggest abattoirs in Andhra Pradesh, slaughters 182,400 cattle every year, animals whose dung could have provided for the fuel needs of 90,000 average Indian families of five. Kerosene imports quadrupled in 1993 from 1988. If livestock were not slaughtered in AP, farmyard manure would cultivate 38,400 hectares producing 530,000 tons of food grain. The state of AP must now spend Rs.9.1 billion to import nitrogen, phosphorous and potash previously provided by livestock over the duration of their lives. The projected earnings of Rs.200 million by Al-Kabeer is actually leading to a drain of billions of rupees in foreign exchange. Finally, in a law-suit against Al-Kabeer, the courts ordered a 50% reduction of its capacity, in order to save the cattle wealth and the rural economy of AP."

An especially anti-democratic move is the recommendation that "animal husbandry Departments under State Govt. should be entrusted with licensing of slaughterhouses as at present, local bodies who are the owners, are also license providers". This proposal essentially asks for the decision-making power to be taken farther away from the people and centralised, so the hassle of manipulating 50 (or so) local bodies in every state could be reduced to that of manipulating just one state department.

> *"More we try to know the about the reasons responsible for the unreasonable increase in the number of slaughterhouses in 'independent' India, the more painful astonishing facts await us. It is like opening a can of worms... It is a conspiracy, political conspiracy to eternalize India's slavery to West's policy of materialism and mammon worship. Sadly, the politicians are successful as the general people are turning more ignorant and immune, gathering themselves in the selfish cocoon of just their own individual happiness. They do not realize that nobody can be an independent individual, however tiny we are a part of BIG network and this is sensitive to the slightest imbalance that we bring in the natural set-up. Smallest of the action has its reaction; and we are paying the price for that."*

The cow has been a symbol of prosperity in India since ancient times and is deeply respected. Indian agriculture is almost philosophically built on integrating cattle into the human lifestyle. Besides helping the farmer, the livestock are the source of many important products (which is different from the factory mindset of man as the 'producer' with the cow just being a machine) - ghee for medicine, dung for fertilizer, milk for food, urine for pesticide and many others.

The Indian farmer has already been pushed to a state of despair by the government's agricultural policies. With the promotion of short stemmed hybrid varieties of paddy and wheat (which have deprived the cattle of their natural feed), agrochemicals, artificial insemination of exotic breeds, hormone injections for more milk production, the government of India has systematically converted the 'localised, environment-friendly, energy- and water-efficient, knowledge-driven agri'culture' into a centralised energy- and water-inefficient, technology- and private-profit-driven agri'business'.

(More information on this issue and an online petition to stop the move towards industrialisation of slaughter is available at www.chennaiorganicfood.com/cow.htm)

So this is our program. Let the cows live. We take sufficient milk. We are getting milk, one thousand pounds. One thousand pounds daily in our, one center, New Vrindaban, Virginia. So we are making various preparations from the milk, and they are very happy, and the cows are also happy. So this is one of our programs, to stop killing this important animal. And the flesh-eaters may wait a little until the cow dies. Then he gets the opportunity. Why there should be slaughterhouse maintained? As you are one of the leading citizens of Paris, we appeal to you to take up this consideration seriously. Why we should maintain slaughterhouse? If we want to eat the flesh, let us wait till the death. And there will be death. There is no doubt about it. So why they should maintain slaughterhouse? And this is most cruelty. A animal which is giving milk, so important foodstuff, and that is being killed, it does not suit any moral sense of any human being.

~ Srila Prabhupada (Room Conversation with Monsieur Mesman, Chief of Law House of Paris — June 11, 1974, Paris)

15.

The New Livestock Policy

A Policy Of Ecocide Of Indigenous Cattle Breeds
And A Policy Of Genocide For India's Small Farmers

by Dr. Vandana Shiva

The Livestock Policy Perspective 1995-2020 developed by the Government of India and the Swiss Development Cooperation is a policy for the destruction of India's farm animal biodiversity and a threat to the survival of small farmers who depend on a diversity based decentralised livestock economy.

India's livestock legacy has four unique dimensions :-

• 1. Cows and bulls are treated as sacred and hence are protected.

• 2. The conservation of farm animals is essential for the sustainability of agriculture and the survival of small farmers.

• 3. The conservation and utilisation of farm animals is based on diversity - both diversity of breeds as well as diversity of function of farm animals

• 4. The sustenance of cattle comes from diverse sources of fodder and feed - agricultural by products such as straw and oil cake, fodder trees planted on farms and common property resources such a village pastures and forests.

Thus, the indigenous approach to livestock is based on diversity, decentralisation, sustainability and equity. Our cattle are not just milk machines or meat machines. They are sentient beings who serve human communities through their multidimensional role in agriculture.

On the other hand, externally driven projects, programmes and policies emerging from industrial societies treat cattle as one-dimensional machines which are maintained with capital intensive and environmentally intensive inputs and which provide a single output - either milk or meat. Polices based on this approach are characterized by monocultures, concentration and centralisation, non-sustainability and inequality.

The new livestock policy has been framed in this paradigm of machines and monocultures. It is a serious attack on principles of

---

Ample food grains can be produced through agricultural enterprises, and profuse supplies of milk, yogurt and ghee can be arranged through cow protection. Abundant honey can be obtained if the forests are protected. Unfortunately, in modern civilization, men are busy killing the cows that are the source of yogurt, milk and ghee, they are cutting down all the trees that supply honey, and they are opening factories to manufacture nuts, bolts, automobiles and wine instead of engaging in agriculture. How can the people be happy? They must suffer from all the misery of materialism. Their bodies become wrinkled and gradually deteriorate until they become almost like dwarves, and a bad odor emanates from their bodies because of unclean perspiration resulting from eating all kinds of nasty things. This is not human civilization. If people actually want happiness in this life and want to prepare for the best in the next life, they must adopt a Vedic civilization.

~ *Srila Prabhuapda (Srimad Bhagavatam 5.16.25)*

diversity, decentralisation, sustainability and equity in the livestock sector.

The Cattle Economy: The Provider For The Poor

The policy document recognizes that the livestock economy is the economy of the poorest households in India.

As stated in Section 2.3: About 630 million people reside in rural areas (74% of total population) of which 40% have incomes which place them below the poverty line. Some 70 million households (73% of total rural households) keep and own livestock of one kind or another and derive on average 20% of their income from this source. Small and marginal fanners and landless tabourers constitute almost two-thirds of these livestock keeping households. The importance of the livestock sector can therefore not be measured purely in terms of its contribution to GDP but it plays a very crucial role in generating income and employment for the weaker sections of the economy. Rapid growth of the livestock sector can be a deciding factor in the efforts at improving nutrition and relieving poverty. Women provide nearly 90% of all labour for livestock management.

However, all the analysis in the policy is totally insensitive to the systems which allow cattle to serve the needs of the poorest. As a result the recommendations are a direct assault on this survival base of the poor.

An Assault on the Culture of Conservation.

The livestock policy paper is disrespectful to the Indian culture of reverence for farm animals. These cultural beliefs are viewed as block to promoting meat production. At a time when meat consumption is going down in western countries themselves, India's livestock policy is trying to convert a predominantly vegetarian

> *Cruelty to dumb animals is one of the distinguishing vices of low and base minds. Wherever it is found, it is a certain mark of ignorance and meanness; a mark which all the external advantages of wealth, splendour, and nobility, cannot obliterate. It is consistent neither with learning nor true civility.*
> ~William Jones

society into a beef eating culture. In the U.S. beef consumption per capita has declined from 88.9 pounds in 1976 to 63.9 pounds in 1990. Cultural attitudes have been the most significant reason for maintaining vegetarian diets for the large majority in India. The livestock policy would like to undermine these conservation policies to promote a meat culture.

As stated in Section 2.10 on Meat Production: The beef production in India is purely an adjunct to milk and draught power production. The animals slaughtered are the old and the infirm and the sterile and are in all cases malnourished. There is no organized marketing and no grading system and beef prices are at a level which makes feeding uneconomic. There is no instance of feedlots or even individual animals being raised for meat. Religious sentiments (particularly in the Northern and Western parts of India) against cattle slaughter seem to spill over also on buffaloes and prevent the utilization of a large number of surplus male calves.

The policy then recommends government interventions to stimulate meat production even though this will totally undermine the basis of sustainable agriculture. (Section 3.10)

Undermining Sustainability Of Agriculture.

The economics of meat exports is totally flawed in a diversity based culture of animal husbandry and farming. Two thirds and more of the power requirements of Indian villages are met by the 80 million work animals. Indian cattle excrete 700 million tons of recoverable manure. Half of which is used as fuel, saving 27 millions

---

Now, we must take to agricultural work -- produce food and give protection to the cows. And if we produce a surplus, we can trade. It is a simple thing that we must do. Our people should live peacefully in farming villages, produce grain and fruit and vegetables, protect the cows, and work hard. And if there is a surplus, we can start restaurants. Krsna conscious people will never be losers by following the instructions of Krsna. They will live comfortably, without any material want, and tyaktva deham punar janma naiti [Bhagavad-gita 4.9]: After leaving this body they will go directly to God. This is our way of life.
~ Srila Prabhupada (JSD 6.5: Slaughterhouse Civilization)

of kerosene, 35 million tons of coal or 68 million tons of wood. The remaining half is used as fertiliser.

As Maneka Gandhi has shown in the case of one export slaughter house, the value of nitrogen, phosphate and potassium provided annually by living cattle is fifty times more than the animal earnings from meat exports, which at current rates of slaughter will wipe out Indian farm animals in 10-15 years. If animals are allowed to live, we will get 19,18,562 tonnes of farmyard manure with the help of their dung and urine.

The livestock policy has nothing to say on the role of animals in the maintenance of sustainability in agriculture. In fact, the livestock policy if implemented would convert cow dung from a source of fertility into a major source of pollution since intensive factory farming of cattle for beef leads to concentration of organic waste from livestock in one place. Since such intensive production is not integrated and cannot be integrated with agriculture as in the case of small farms with decentralised livestock economies, the animal waste turns into a pollutant. Nitrogen from cattle waste is converted into Ammonia and Nitrates which leach into and pollute the surface and ground water.

A feedlot of 10,000 cattle produces. as much waste as a city of 110,000 people. This is the reason the Netherlands has been able to export its toxic cow dung to India and is unable to reintegrate this animal waste into its own agricultural systems. Cow dung is a fertilizer only in small scale integrated farming systems. In large scale, concentrated and specialised factory farming systems, this wealth is converted into a hazardous waste. Further, since intensive factory farming of cattle goes hand in hand with intensive feeding and feed production which in turn requires heavy use of fertilizers and pesticides, the cattle waste from factory farms is very heavily contaminated with chemicals.

Animal Energy.

While in decentralised small scale animal husbandry, cow dung is the most significant gift of the cow to sustainable agriculture, there is total neglect of the contribution of cattle to renewal of soil fertility in the livestock policy. While reference is made to draught power, it is only with the objective of wiping out this source of sustainable energy production, without recognising that if animals were replaced by tractors in India we would have to spend more than a thousand million US dollars annually on fossil fuels, worsening our debt crisis and our balance of payment. In total indifference to the huge economic costs to both farmers and the country generated by substituting animal energy by fossil fuel run mechanical energy, the livestock policy blindly proposes such a shift.

As Section 2.4 on Drought Power: The number of work animals continued to increase through 1977 but has since fallen by about 10 million to a level of 70 million in 1987 of which 9% are buffaloes. To ensure replacement every sixth year one needs about 0.67 breedable cows per bullock. The bullocks have been largely replaced by mechanical means in transport and irrigation and are now almost exclusively u@ for land preparation. How much of the gross cropped area (180 m ha) that is cultivated by animal power is uncertain (an estimate of 60 m ha is given in a recent WB report) but it is clear that the bullocks may only be utilized for a short period of the year (at most 100 days). Since bullocks generally are not put out to grazing except possibly during the slack season, feeding them and the necessary replacement stock imposes a major strain. Crossbreds are generally not appreciated as bullocks. Although there are opportunities to introduce improved bullock genes in F2 and subsequent crosses these are seldom utilized. In larger herds one may use some cows for crossbreeding while others are used for bullock (and marginal milk) production. In smaller herds one can however not separately pursue both the power and the dairy objective. The policy of upgrading bullocks and introducing improved implements has met with limited success (some implements like the seeder has been introduced). Where the field sizes, topography etc. allow the farmer has the choice between keeping his own bullocks (and the stock

needed for their replacement), disposing of the bullocks and either hire power for cultivation (animal or tractor) with the consequent risk that the timeliness of operations will suffer, or acquiring a tractor and offer its service for transport and cultivation. We have only limited material that illustrates the relative attractiveness of these options for different farm sizes with due consideration to the importance of timeliness of land preparation (see however Sharma and Binswanger). The trend is obviously away from animal power.

As stated in Section 5.2 on Interventions: with respect of animal power further adds, if our aim, as suggested, is to accelerate the trend towards mechanization as well as to promote upgrading of bullock power and improvement of implements we will need to consider interventions for this purpose.

In order to accelerate mechanization one may consider providing credit for tractor (incl.equipment) procurement and to make sure (through training programs and subsidy) that the weaker sections get a fair chance to exploit this opportunity. At a time when as a result of the climate change crisis we should be moving away from fossil fuel use to sustainable sources of energy, the livestock policy recommends the reverse.

It also neglects the fact that even in the affluent state of Punjab, farmers are shifting back from tractors to bullocks because the

tractors have become too expensive to operate due to rise in fuel prices.

The Flawed One-Dimensional, Linear And Monoculture Logic

The livestock policy is based on a flawed logic of one dimensionality and linearity. One dimensional thinking is based on perceiving cattle as linear and mechanical input-output systems with a single function, single output usually limited to milk or meat. Linearity is displayed in treating these inputs and outputs as linear flows. *On this one dimensional and linear logic, it says that India's 70 million work animals have to be fed and managed over a "365 day feeding year" while they give a "100 day working year". On the basis of this flawed logic it is then stated that these "inefficient" work animals can become progressively redundant to the farming sector and cattle population can be reduced to one third of what it is.*

This concept of efficiency applied to cattle is totally misplaced. Firstly, for most rural families, animals are part of their extended families and are not mere work machines. If this misplaced logic of efficiency had to be applied to humans, we too should be totally annihilated and replaced by robots because humans are "inefficient" as they have to be looked after in childhood and old age and during ill health, while they "work" only in adult life and during healthy periods. Treating humans and animals as if they were mere machines with an externally defined single function is ethically outrageous and economically flawed.

Secondly, in any case, in India, farm animals are not single output, single function machines. They have many functions only one of which is to provide work energy. Even when work animals are not pulling ploughs or bullock carts they are giving manure, the most significant contribution that cattle make to agriculture. Thirdly, a comparative energy audit of inputs and useful outputs from U.S. cattle and Indian cattle shows that Indian cattle are far more efficient than their counterparts in industrial economies in using energy. They use 29 per cent of organic matter provided to them, and 22 per cent of the energy and 3 per cent of the protein in contrast to 9, 7 and 5 per cent respectively in the intensive cattle industry in the U.S.

Indian cattle provide food in the excess of the edible food consumed, in contrast to the U.S. where 6 times as much edible food is fed to the cattle as is obtained from them.

It is this wasteful and inefficient system of livestock management that the new livestock policy introduced in India in the name of improving "efficiency" of cattle.

Undermining Farm Animal Biodiversity.

The Biodiversity Convention obliges all member states to protect biodiversity. This includes farm animal biodiversity- India's indigenous livestock policy has been based on a wide diversity of cattle breeds. They are high milk yielders like the Gir, Sindhi, Sahiwal and Deoni. They are dual purpose breeds such as the Haryana, Ongole, Gaolao, Krishna Valley, 'Ibarparkar, Kankrej. Finally there are specialised draught animals such as Nagori, Bachour, Kenkatha, Malvi, Kherigarh, Hallikar, Amritmohal, Kangayam, Khillari etc.

The livestock policy document totally fails to address the issue of conservation of animal biodiversity even though it has been drafted after the Biodiversity Convention was signed. In fact, by recommending the wiping out of draught power, the policy is indirectly writing a death certificate for indigenous breeds which have been evolved as dual purpose breeds for both dairy and drought power or a specialised draught animals. By a one dimensional focus on dairy and meat alone, and a deliberate destruction of the animal energy economy, the policy promotes the replacement of diverse indigenous breeds by uniform breeds from

Moreover, demons must always do the opposite of the demigods. That is their nature. We have actually seen this in relation to our Krsna consciousness movement. We are advocating cow protection and encouraging people to drink more milk and eat palatable preparations made of milk, but the demons, just to protest such proposals, are claiming that they are advanced in scientific knowledge, as described here by the words svadhyaya-sruta-sampannah. They say that according to their scientific way, they have discovered that milk is dangerous and that the beef obtained by killing cows is very nutritious.

~Srimad Bhagavatam 8.7.3

Europe. One-dimensional thinking thus leads to a monoculture of farm animals bred and maintained through external imported inputs for an export oriented economy.

Aggravating The Fodder Crisis.

The primary reason for decline of cattle is the shortage of fodder. The fodder crisis has three roots - one lies in agriculture policy based on Green Revolution technologies which undermined the sources of fodder from agricultural crops. High Yielding Varieties were bred for grain and led to decline in fodder.

The second source of the fodder crisis lies in aid programmes such as "social forestry" and "farm forestry" projects which promoted the planting of monocultures of non-fodder species such as Eucalyptus, thus aggravating the shortage of fodder.

> *Some rascals put forward the theory that an animal has no soul or is something like dead stone. In this way they rationalize that there is no sin in animal killing. Actually animals are not dead stone, but the killers of animals are stone-hearted. Consequently no reason or philosophy appeals to them. They continue keeping slaughterhouses and killing animals.   -Srila Prabhupada (Srimad-Bhagavatam 4.26.9)*

Finally, the enclosure of the commons has also led to scarcity of grazing lands and pastures. In addition there has been a scarcity of cattle feed both because traditional sources of cattle feed such as oil cakes have declined as a result of the Green Revolution which displaced oil seeds and because new sources such as soya bean cake are largely exported. The Agricultural Minister recently announced that he wanted a special port set up for the export of soya bean cake.

Industrial countries such as Netherlands use seven times more land than their own in Third World countries for fodder and feed to provide inputs to their intensive factory farming. The livestock policy does recognise the crisis of fodder and feed in India but fails to provide solutions. In fact, by promoting intensive factory farming, it is indirectly proposing a system that will intensify the pressure on land, divert land from food for people to food to animals and further erode the scarce environmental resources of the country.

As Section 2.7 states: The feed and fodder resources are of course shared by all livestock. Lactating cows and bullocks receive preferential treatment while sheep and goats, dry and unproductive animals and backyard poultry to a large extent have to fend for themselves. Agricultural residues are currently estimated to provide 40%, grazing 31%, green fodder (cut and cultivated) 26%, and grain and concentrates (mainly for commercial poultry and high producing cows) 3% of total consumption. Over the last decade the straw grain ratio has deteriorated because of the large scale adoption of high yielding varieties which also produce poorer quality straw.

So without being devotee a man will become cruel, cruel, cruel, cruel, cruel, in this way go to hell. And devotee cannot tolerate. We have studied in the life of Lord Jesus Christ. When he saw that in the Jewish synagogue the birds were being killed, he became shocked. He therefore left. Jesus... He inaugurated the Christian religion. Perhaps you know. He was shocked by this animal-killing. And therefore his first commandment is "Thou shall not kill." But the foolish Christians, instead of following his instruction, they are opening daily slaughterhouses.

~ Srila Prabhupada (Srimad-Bhagavatam 7.9.52 — Vrndavana, April 7, 1976)

As Section 2.8 states: The amount of common property grazing land has deteriorated sharply from 78m ha in 1950-51 to 55 m ha in 1988-89 (admittedly very crude estimates) together with the quality of grazing in the remaining areas. This has been at least partly compensated by encroachment into reserved forest areas (67m ha) a large proportion of which (probably more than 50%) now exhibit serious degradation (other factors than grazing may have contributed to this state of affairs).

Cultivated green fodder is estimated at 7 million ha and is gaining in importance (particularly in the NW). The nutritional constraints in dairy production are very real and the conditions under which stall-feeding, concentrate feeding and cultivated fodder become viable options are not very clear.

There is no recommendation in the policy that would improve the natural resource and environmental base for ameliorating the fodder scarcity. Steps in this direction would include:

a) Shift to agricultural crops and crop varieties that produce food for both animals and humans. For example, our seed conservation programme, 'Navadanya' has shown that high fodder yielding varieties are the most popular ones among the farmers.

b) Shift to fodder trees in agroforestry and social forestry programmes.

c) Recover and rejuvenate the commons

d) Stop export of cattle feed.

The policy perspective has no recommendations with respect to (a, b and d) above. With respect to c, it recommends the opposite of what the environment movements have been saying.

As Section 3.4 states:

We are doubtful about the chances of success in relation to the village common (panchayat) lands and would not recommend any major effort to establish management for and to regenerate this resource.

The Government Livestock Policy developed in collaboration with the Swiss Development Corporation is thus the opposite of what an ecologically sound animal husbandry policy should be given the information we now have about the ecological and social externalities of intensive factory farming of animals. Instead of promoting the conservation of indigenous breeds of cattle, the policy prescribes the wiping out of local breeds. Instead of reducing dependence on fossil fuels, the policy recommends replacing ploughs and bullock carts with tractors. Instead of promoting reduction of meat eating it promotes increase of meat production. Instead of recovering the commons it suggests we should let the commons disappear.

This is a prescription for wiping out biodiversity and worsening the climate change crisis. Both the Indian government and the Swiss government are thus acting against their commitments made at the Earth Summit in Rio, in Agenda 21 as well as in the Biodiversity Convention and the Climate Change Convention.

The official policy needs to be totally revised to reflect people's concern, government obligations and full scientific and ecological knowledge that is available about the environmental and economic costs of large scale, centralised and intensive factory farming.

The People's Ecological Agenda.

For the livestock policy to be ecologically sound and socially just the following elements must be urgently addressed.

1. Protection of native breeds and conservation of animal biodiversity.

2. Strengthening the role of farm animals in sustainable agriculture.

3. Stopping the slaughter of cattle for exports.

4. Stopping the export of oil cake and cattle feed.

5. Taking urgent steps to improve the fodder situation through planting appropriate crop species and trees and by rejuvenating the commons.

6. Preventing the import of environmentally unsound methods of intensive factory farming of animals which degrade and pollute the environment and cause health hazards to consumers.

16.

Cow Raids

The Most Lucrative Profession In India

A visitor to India is taken aback by the sight of cows walking unattended or lounging in the busy streets. The traffic skirts round them taking extreme care not to disturb their walk or nap. Cows of all ages roam wherever they like. Some cows are so old that they can hardly stand. But nobody would dare to push them or use a stick to move them from the busiest of intersections.

But these street roaming cows, India's trademark, may soon be history. All over India, butchers have started raiding towns and villages to kidnap cows, both stray as well as privately owned. Government's export policy has made cattle rustling one of the most lucrative businesses today. In each raid, they stand to make lakhs of rupees as each head can fetch upto 10,000 rupees. A dead cow in India now commands better price than a living one.

We only mention a few cases here for the sake of reference. Hundreds of such cases are reported every month from different parts of India.

The Activities Of Butchers In Braja

By Antony Brennan

A recent 'Care for Cows in Vrindavan' newsletter from Kurma Rupa das highlights an issue that warrants the attention of all of us: the increased incidence of cows being kidnapped in Vrindavan and sold for profit.

In the March newsletter (careforcows.org) Kurma Rupa tells about those who make their living by abducting cows for slaughter. He refers to them as butchers.

As if this isn't bad enough there are also accomplices that "pose as sympathisers and offer support but only with intent to win our confidence so they can learn of our plans and thus weaken our defences," Kurma says.

Reportedly the kidnappers can receive up to 10,000 rupees for a single cow. According to villagers the kidnappers are becoming more brazen and better organised. Authorities have done little to prevent the abductions and locals are risking their lives trying to prevent the deadly night raids. "Sorry to say, but it seems that the values of the elite of modern India have changed. It is no longer the cow who is sacred, but it is profit that is sacred. Cow protection is being replaced by profit protection," Kurma Rupa says.

Security had not previously required great effort or resources as cow protection programs once received genuine support from all quarters. Now things are changing and the security of cows requires maximum effort.

In the Match newsletter Kurma Rupa paints a disturbing picture and outlines a shocking chain of events.

"On the cold, damp and foggy night of January 2, 2009 a truck with five or six men stopped in front or our gate. They were armed

These saintly kings gave protection to all the prajas, or living beings, to live and to fulfill their terms of embodiment. Maharaja Pariksit was actually an ideal saintly king because while touring his kingdom he happened to see that a poor cow was about to be killed by the personified Kali, whom he at once took to task as a murderer. This means that even the animals were given protection by the saintly administrators, not from any sentimental point of view, but because those who have taken their birth in the material world have the right to live.

~ Srila Prabhupada (Srimad Bhagavatam 1.12.19)

and hostile and arrived with intent to steal our cows. One of them demanded that our guard surrender the keys to the gate but he secured himself upstairs.

The intruders jumped the gate and performed a thorough search of our facility. Since our cows are not tied up they moved about restlessly in the fog, filling the night with the frantic ringing of their bells.

The thieves next broke the lock on our front gate but then mysteriously left without taking anything. We reported the incident to the local police and they advised us to hire two gunmen. Several of us volunteered to stand guard as well. We were supplied two men armed with shotguns for the next month.

Kurma Rupa says the hired men turned out to have little interest in protecting the cows. Their weapons were poorly maintained and ineffective. Eventually the gunmen were fired.

"In any case the break-in and frustration with the hired guards had a unifying affect on the volunteer go-sevaks at Care for Cows." Kurma Rupa says. Volunteers began taking shifts to protect the cows each night. "Neighbours gave us their phone numbers and invited us to call them in the middle of the night in the case of an emergency and wealthy businessman from Delhi donated flood lights and pledged to arrange siren to distract and scare off any intruders."

At the end of January Care for Cows was reasonably secure. "We received several reports that cows were being stolen in other places around the town," Kurma Rupa says. "We got permission from the local police to patrol the streets by motorcycle as a service to the rest of the community. Every night two or three of our volunteers patrol areas that street cows frequent and at times we are accompanied by police or concerned residents with gun permits. Our objective is to locate the butchers, notify the police and then help chase them out of town."

In February Kurma Rupa learned that two trucks and fifteen men armed with the guns had come to abduct cows. Six armed

Our inhumane treatment of livestock is becoming widespread and more and more barbaric... These creatures feel; they know pain. They suffer pain just as we humans feel pain.
- *Senator Robert Byrd*

men jumped out of the trucks and loudly announced that if anyone came out of their Houses they would meet with death. Five other men forced several street cows on their truck by prodding them with swords. Several men rode in the back of the truck poised to shoot or throw rocks at anyone who attempted to pursue them out of town. "It is interesting to note that this incident took place hardly two hundred meters away from the local police station," Kurma Rupa says.

Volunteers at Care for Cows and other local villagers and well wishers have participated in several confrontations with those who come to steal the cows to be slaughtered for profit. On these occasions the group have been successful in chasing off the dangerous and armed abductors, but not without risk.

"It is most unfortunate that cow protection today in Krishna's holy land means that one has to risk his life to keep them from being abducted for slaughter," Kurma Rupa says.

Devotees and well wishers who wish to help should contact Uttar Pradesh government ministers and demand action be taken against those who kidnap and kill cows. Letters can be faxed to the Chief Minister at the following fax number: +91 522 2237620.

Kidnapping of cows is a criminal offence In Vrindavan. Residents of Vrindavan say the villagers and cows need support and protection whilst the police need resources to stop and catch those who prey on the cows.

If you wish you can send your letter by email to dontkillcows@gmail.com. All the letters sent to this email address will be collected and presented to the Chief Minister with a petition asking his government to take action.

A king or ruler is meant to treat all the living beings in his kingdom as his own self or children. The subjects also lovingly treated the king as their father.

In this age, however, so-called kings and presidents do not treat all other living entities as their own self. Most of them are meat-eaters, and even though they may not be meat-eaters and may pose themselves to be very religious and pious, they still allow cow slaughter within their state.
~ Srila Prabhupada (Srimad Bhagavatam 6.7.24)

How Vrindavan Is Losing Its Cows To Slaughter

By Antony Brennan

Subhangi Devi Dasi lives in Vrindavan, India. Recently she was awoken early in the morning to witness a site none of us would even dream could be happening. Krishna's cows are being violently kidnapped in the night. It is believed the cows are killed and sold for their flesh and leather products.

"I was sleeping," Subhangi Devi Dasi says. "At 2.00 am I hear cows crying, people screaming and yelling. I run out to my balcony and see a truck backing away and cows franticly running in all directions down the lanes, all crying. I have never seen that in Vrindavan."

Subhangi was witnessing the kidnapping of the local cows. "Then I see some local men throwing stones at the trucks and swearing in Hindi, some other men came with machetes and one with a rifle," Subhangi

says. These men were coming to protect the cows "The truck backed out of the road and drove off."

Arjuna, one of the men trying to protect the cows says the kidnappers came with several trucks. "They caught and stole 48 cows just here in this area," he says. "The men were ruthless, throwing the cows in the back of their trucks, beating then and in some cases killing them if they were resisting," Arjuna says. "Blood was everywhere."

Villagers say the kidnappers are armed and attack anyone who tries to stop them. "A month or so back." Arjuna says. "The police put up barricades to try to stop the kidnappers. That night they rammed the barricades with their trucks."

"It is so out of control," says Arjuna. "Vrindavan is the land of cows and these demons have become aware that there are so many cows and goshallas just ripe for the picking." The locals are helpless. They can do little without risking their own lives.

It is reported that 15 days ago, when the police tried to stop them, the kidnappers rammed a police jeep. A policeman fired a shot and he got a rock in the head for his effort. It is reported that the police had to pull back as there were only four of them, whilst there were eight heavily armed kidnappers. "They criminals seem to be aware of how much resistance they will encounter and come prepared to meet it," Arjuna says.

"Sometimes they hit the cows in the head with rocks and sometimes shoot them or hack them with machetes if they resist," says Arjuna. "They used to come in one truck now they travel with four trucks at a time."

Subhangi Devi Dasi says she has heard the cows can fetch up to 10,000 rupees. It is no wonder kidnappers are armed and are prepared to injure even the police. Villagers who try to prevent the kidnappings are said to be placing themselves and their families in a very dangerous situation.

My comments: I'm writing with a heavy heart. After reading this article, I was motionless for sometime and still in shock. I don't know how such incidents keep happening. Vrindavan residents should be aggressive and do something concrete (large-scale strike/road-blocking, notifying media houses) to bring the attention of the nation. If this is not immediately stopped, those murderers will increase their activities.

Ahmedabad Crime Round Up: 25 Cows Stolen In One Night

Monday, Oct 1, 2012, Agency: DNA

In his application with Aslali police on Sunday, Ishwar Rabari said that a 20-strong gang stole his 25 cows late on Saturday night.

Rabari, who hails from Bevdi village of Daskroi taluka, alleged that the gang came in seven vehicles, including mini-trucks and jeeps and broke into the cow shelter adjoining his house.

They tranquilised the cows and hauled them away in the trucks. The incident happened at about 2.30am on Sunday.

Rabari woke up hearing the noise and came out of his house, only to spot the goons run away with the cattle. He gathered other villagers and chased them but the gang was well equipped to handle any such situation.

They pelted stones at the villagers and managed to escape into the darkness in the ensuing melee.

Police sub-inspector with Aslali, DL Dodia has launched investigations in the case.

Gurgaon - 7 Cops Beaten Up By Villagers

Sanjay Yadav, Times News Network, Apr 3, 2012,

Seven policemen were beaten up mercilessly by villagers after they failed to stop cow smugglers early on Monday morning at the Kaliyawas village police barrier. After driving away the policemen, the villagers also blocked the Gurgaon-Badli road near Makdola village.

After getting assurance from ACP (Sadar) Krishna Murari that action will be taken against the cops, the villagers ended the road blockade. Sources said that all the seven cops were suspended on the charge of dereliction of duty and transferred to Police Lines, Gurgaon. Police officials did not confirm the cops' suspension and transfer yet.

According to the police, the incident took place at the Kaliyawas village police barrier around 3AM on Monday. The barrier was installed for the prevention and detection of crime by the Gurgaon crime branch near Kaliyawas village of Farrukhnagar. At this barrier seven cops were deployed. They were EASI Chander Singh, Raghunath, constable Naresh, Dinesh, Sudesh, Roshan, Mahipal and Vijay.

According to the villagers, six to seven cow smugglers were seen rushing to the village in a max open jeep late on Sunday night. When villagers wanted to know the reason, they could not give a satisfactory answer and started to flee from the village. In the meantime, on the doubt, two villagers followed them on a bike, and were hit by stones thrown from the jeep by the cow smugglers.

The villagers on the bike then took the help of a truck driver who was in a dhaba on the way. The truck driver helped them give chase in his truck but cops stopped the truck at the barrier and helped the cow smugglers escape with ease.

That enraged the villagers who went on the rampage and beat up the policemen. The rest of the police force fled the spot. Some hours after that, the villagers sat on a dharna on the Gurgaon-Badli road, causing a massive traffic jam.

When police reinforcements reached the spot and the ACP spoke to them, villagers agreed to end their blockade. Meanwhile, villagers also alleged that cattle theft had increased in the area and police were not lodging any complaint.

UP IPS Officer Shunted Out For Exposing Minister In Cow Smuggling

By Niticentral Staff on February 7, 2013

Gonda superintendent of police Navneet Kumar Rana, who exposed senior Samajwadi Party leader KC Pandey offering bribe for the release of culprits caught in trafficking cows for slaughter, has been shunted out by the Uttar Pradesh Government.

Pandey figured in a sting operation of cattle smuggling carried out by Rana.

But now, the many rascals heading the government allow animal slaughter. When Maharaja Pariksit saw a degraded man trying to kill a cow, he immediately drew his sword and said, "Who are you? Why are you trying to kill this cow?" He was a real king. Nowadays, unqualified men have taken the presidential post. And although they may pose themselves as very religious, they are simply rascals. Why? Because under their noses thousands of cows are being killed, while they collect a good salary. Any leader who is at all religious should resign his post in protest if cow slaughter goes on under his rule. Since people do not know that these administrators are rascals, they are suffering. And the people are also rascals because they are voting for these bigger rascals. It is Plato's view that the government should be ideal, and this is the ideal: The saintly philosophers should be at the head of the state; according to their advice the politicians should rule.

~ *Srila Prabhupada (Journey of Self Discovery 7.1)*

On December 29, 2012, Gonda police seized a truck carrying a consignment of cows in Khargapur.

Rana had alleged that SP national secretary KC Pandey, who enjoys the status of a Minister of State as vice-chairman of UP Council of Sugarcane Research, had allegedly offered bribe for leaving the seized truck.

It is noted that Chief Minister Akhilesh Yadav had assured "proper inquiry" after the issue came to the light and promised action against the traffickers.

Meanwhile, the UP Government has transferred the probe into the cattle smuggling case to CB-CID.

THE AUTHOR

Dr. Sahadeva dasa (Sanjay Shah) is a monk in Vaisnava
tradition. His areas of work include research in Vedic and
contemporary thought, Corporate and educational training,
social work and counselling, travelling, writing books and of
course, practicing spiritual life and spreading awareness about
the same.

He is also an accomplished musician, composer, singer,
instruments player and sound engineer. He has more than a
dozen albums to his credit so far. (SoulMelodies.com) His
varied interests include alternative holistic living, Vedic
studies, social criticism, environment, linguistics, history, art
& crafts, nature studies, web technologies etc.

Many of his books have been acclaimed internationally and
translated in other languages.

By The Same Author

Oil-Final Countdown To A Global Crisis And Its Solutions

End of Modern Civilization And Alternative Future

To Kill Cow Means To End Human Civilization

Cow And Humanity - Made For Each Other

Cows Are Cool - Love 'Em!

Let's Be Friends - A Curious, Calm Cow

Wondrous Glories of Vraja

We Feel Just Like You Do

Tsunami Of Diseases Headed Our Way - Know Your Food Before Time Runs Out

Cow Killing And Beef Export - The Master Plan To Turn India Into A Desert

Capitalism Communism And Cowism - A New Economics For The 21st Century

Noble Cow - Munching Grass, Looking Curious And Just Hanging Around

World - Through The Eyes Of Scriptures

To Save Time Is To Lengthen Life

Life Is Nothing But Time - Time Is Life, Life Is Time

Lost Time Is Never Found Again

Spare Us Some Carcasses - An Appeal From The Vultures

An Inch of Time Can Not Be Bought With A Mile of Gold

Career Women - The Violence of Modern Jobs And The Lost Art of Home Making

Cow Dung – A Down To Earth Solution To Global Warming And Climate Change

Corporatocracy - You Are A Corporate Citizen, A Slave of Invisible And Ruthless Masters

Working Moms And Rise of A Lost Generation

Glories of Thy Wondrous Name

Cow Dung For Food Security And Survival of Human Race

As Long As There Are Slaughterhouses, There Will Be Wars

Peak Soil – Industrial Civilization, On The Verge of Eating Itself

If Violence Must Stop, Slaughterhouses Must Close Down

(More information on availability on DrDasa.com)